ARMY, MARINE CORPS, NAVY, AIR FORCE

TECHINT

MULTI-SERVICE TACTICS, TECHNIQUES, AND PROCEDURES FOR TECHNICAL INTELLIGENCE OPERATIONS

FM 2-22.401

NTTP 2-01.4

AFTTP(I)

3-2.63

AIR LAND SEA APPLICATION CENTER

JUNE 2006

DISTRIBUTION RESTRICTION:
Approved for public release; distribution is unlimited.

MULTI-SERVICE TACTICS, TECHNIQUES, AND PROCEDURES

FOREWORD

This publication has been prepared under our direction for use by our respective commands and other commands as appropriate.

DAVID A. FASTABEND
Major General, US Army
Deputy Director/Chief of Staff
    Army Capabilities Integration
    Center

R.T. NOLAN
Rear Admiral, USN
Commander
Navy Warfare Development
    Command

JAMES F. JACKSON
Brigadier General, USAF
Commander
Headquarters Air Force
    Doctrine Center

This publication is available through the ALSA Web site (www.alsa.mil); through the Army at Army Knowledge Online (AKO) (www.us.army.mil) and at the General Dennis J. Reimer Training and Doctrine Digital Library (www.train.army.mil) Web sites; and through the Air Force at the Air Force Publishing Web site (www.e-publishing.af.mil).

PREFACE

1. Purpose

This publication provides a common set of multi-Service tactics, techniques, and procedures (MTTP) for technical intelligence (TECHINT) operations. It serves as a reference for Service TECHINT planners and operators to build and execute coordinated multi-Service TECHINT operations. It provides guidance to tactical forces on the evacuation of captured materiel that has intelligence value. Additionally, it informs the joint force commanders (JFCs) and their staffs about the missions, requirements, and capabilities of TECHINT forces and essential information to effectively employ and utilize TECHINT capabilities.

2. Scope

This publication guides planners through the process of requesting, deploying, and employing the unique, highly specialized, and mission enhancing expertise of multi-Service TECHINT teams. It is designed for planners at all levels and defines methods to ensure TECHINT capabilities are fully integrated and utilized to the maximum extent possible to provide captured enemy equipment identification, assessment, collection, exploitation, and evacuation in support of national technical intelligence requirements. This publication:

- Supplements established doctrine and tactics, techniques and procedures (TTP).
- Provides reference material to assist ground forces on the evacuation of captured material of intelligence value.
- Assists in planning and conducting TECHINT operations.
- Promotes an understanding of the complexities of TECHINT operations.
- Incorporates TTP, lessons learned, and the latest information available on TECHINT operations.

3. Applicability

This multi-Service publication provides tactical guidance for commanders and staffs of the Army, Navy, and Air Force.

4. Implementation Plan

Participating Service command offices of primary responsibility (OPRs) will review this publication, validate the information and, where appropriate, reference and incorporate it in Service manuals, regulations, and curricula as follows:

Army. Upon approval and authentication, this publication incorporates the procedures contained herein into the United States (US) Army Doctrine and Training Literature Program as directed by the Commander, US Army Training and Doctrine Command (TRADOC). Distribution is in accordance with applicable directives and the Initial Distribution Number (IDN) listed on the authentication page.

Navy. The Navy will incorporate these procedures in US Navy training and doctrine publications as directed by the Commander, Navy Warfare Development Command (NWDC)[N5]. Distribution is in accordance with Military Standard Requisition and Issue Procedure Desk Guide (MILSTRIP Desk Guide) Navy Supplement Publication-409 (NAVSUP P-409).

Air Force. The Air Force will incorporate the procedures in this publication in accordance with applicable governing directives. Distribution is in accordance with Air Force Instruction (AFI) 33-360.

5. User Information

a. TRADOC, NWDC, Headquarters AFDC, and the Air Land Sea Application (ALSA) Center developed this publication with the joint participation of the approving Service commands. ALSA will review and update this publication as necessary.

b. This publication reflects current joint and Service doctrine, command and control organizations, facilities, personnel, responsibilities, and procedures. Changes in Service protocol, appropriately reflected in joint and Service publications, will likewise be incorporated in revisions to this document.

c. We encourage recommended changes for improving this publication. Key your comments to the specific page and paragraph and provide a rationale for each recommendation. Send comments and recommendations directly to—

Army

Commander, US Army Training and Doctrine Command
ATTN: ATFC-RD
Fort Monroe VA 23651-5000
DSN 680-3951 COMM (757) 788-3951
E-mail: doctrine@monroe.army.mil

Navy

Commander, Navy Warfare Development Command
ATTN: N5
686 Cushing Road
Newport RI 02841-1207
DSN 948-1070/4201 COMM (401) 841-1070/4201
E-mail: alsapubs@nwdc.navy.mil

Air Force

Commander, Air Force Doctrine Center
ATTN: DJ
155 North Twining Street
Maxwell AFB AL 36112-6112
DSN 493-2640/2256 COMM (334) 953-2640/2256
E-mail: afdc.dj@maxwell.af.mil

ALSA

Director, ALSA Center
114 Andrews Street
Langley AFB VA 23665-2785
DSN 575-0902 COMM (757) 225-0902
E-mail: alsa.director@langley.af.mil

FM 2-22.401

NTTP 2-01.4

AFTTP(I) 3-2.63

US Army Training and Doctrine Command
Fort Monroe, Virginia
Navy Warfare Development Command
Newport, Rhode Island
Headquarters, Air Force Doctrine Center
Maxwell Air Force Base, Alabama

9 June 2006

TECHINT

MULTI-SERVICE TACTICS, TECHNIQUES, AND PROCEDURES FOR TECHNICAL INTELLIGENCE OPERATIONS

TABLE OF CONTENTS

TABLES

This page intentionally left blank.

EXECUTIVE SUMMARY

TECHINT

Multi-Service Tactics, Techniques, and Procedures for Technical Intelligence Operations

When established by a Joint Task Force Commander, the Captured Materiel Exploitation Center (CMEC) conducts TECHINT operations against enemy air, sea, and ground forces in combat and contingency operations and participates in related peacetime training activities such as exercises and war games where technical intelligence applies.

TECHINT includes the identification, assessment, collection, exploitation, and evacuation of captured enemy materiel (CEM) in support of national and immediate technical intelligence requirements. The technical intelligence acquired through CMEC operations provides rapid performance and vulnerability assessments of enemy equipment, giving a critical edge to US forces in current and future operations.

The process for conducting TECHINT operations in a multi-Service environment begins at the Service level. The Army and Air Force have dedicated TECHINT units to support CMEC operations. In addition, each Service possesses TECHINT personnel to provide support, augmentation, and subject matter expertise to CMEC operations. These units and personnel receive specialized training to effectively operate in hostile and austere environments.

The unified commands play a major role in TECHINT tasking. Each unified command should have a designated TECHINT planner within the intelligence directorate (J-2) to coordinate requirements with national intelligence production centers and the joint staff. TECHINT is an intelligence mission assigned to the J-2, who is responsible for CMEC activities. The CMEC executes mission assignments based on immediate wartime support requirements in addition to national collection requirements priorities. The J-2 coordinates support for CMEC missions with the Defense Intelligence Agency (DIA), and then coordinates with each Service through command channels to provide forces, capabilities, and support as required. The CMEC commander reports directly to the J-2 to integrate new technical intelligence into current joint force intelligence reports.

PROGRAM PARTICIPANTS

The following commands and agencies participated in the development of this publication:

Joint

US Joint Forces Command, Norfolk, VA
Defense Intelligence Agency (Pentagon), Alexandria, VA
Missile and Space Intelligence Center, Huntsville, AL

Army

US Army Training and Doctrine Command, Fort Monroe, VA
National Ground Intelligence Center, Charlottesville, VA
203d Military Intelligence Battalion, Aberdeen Proving Ground, MD

Navy

Navy Warfare Development Command (Norfolk Detachment), Norfolk, VA
Office of Naval Intelligence, Washington, DC

Air Force

Air Force Doctrine Center, ATTN: DJ, Maxwell AFB, AL
Air Intelligence Agency, Lackland AFB, TX
National Air and Space Intelligence Center, Wright-Patterson AFB, OH

Chapter I

TECHINT OVERVIEW

1. Introduction

a.   Joint Publication (JP) 1-02 defines technical intelligence as "Intelligence derived from exploitation of foreign material, produced for strategic, operational, and tactical level commanders. Technical intelligence begins when an individual Service member finds something new on the battlefield and takes the proper steps to report it. The item is then exploited at succeedingly higher levels until a countermeasure is produced to neutralize the adversary's technological advantage."

b.   The TECHINT mission is to:

(1) Prevent technological surprise and maintain US technological advantage against any adversary.

(2) Provide the combatant commander with intelligence to effectively enhance awareness of the enemy and force protection measures.

(3) Develop and employ effective countermeasures to defeat enemy weapon systems and TTP.

(4) Provide tailored, timely, and accurate TECHINT support to the warfighter throughout the entire range of military operations.

(5) Execute technical reconnaissance and assessment of enemy equipment and capability; confirm or deny enemy order of battle.

c.   TECHINT, as an intelligence product, is dependent on the timely employment of TECHINT teams, and the subsequent collection, exploitation, and analysis of foreign warfighting equipment and associated materiel. At the strategic level, the exploitation and interpretation of foreign weapon systems, materiel, and technologies are referred to as scientific and technical intelligence (S&TI). S&TI covers:

(1) Foreign developments in basic and applied research and in applied engineering techniques.

(2) Scientific and technical (S&T) characteristics, capabilities, and limitations of all foreign military systems, weapons, weapon systems, and materiel.

(3) Research and development (R&D) related to these systems and the production methods employed for their manufacture.

d.   Employment of the Captured Materiel Exploitation Center (CMEC) during war and contingencies supports these TECHINT goals and missions by the:

(1) Exploitation of captured or defecting enemy materiel and supporting documentation.

(2) Exploitation of known enemy foreign materiel and targets of opportunity by all appropriate and available means.

2. TECHINT Support to the Warfighter

a.   Operational and Tactical Level. Operational and tactical commanders rely on technological advantage to successfully synchronize and execute complex modern operations. The introduction of a surprise technological capability by an adversary causes confusion and delays mission accomplishment until the capability is understood and countered. TECHINT is the key to the early identification of an adversary's technical capabilities, vulnerabilities, and intent. Technical intelligence provides the information for the development and employment of countermeasures by the operational and tactical commander. TECHINT is a valuable force enabler to the commander.

b.   Strategic Level. The US has relied on its military strength and industrial infrastructure as a strategic deterrent to war. The strength of the US military lies, in part, in the diversity and extent of its technology base. While the US aspires to be the leader in integrating technology, the actual products are available to any buyer. An adversary can achieve temporary technological parity or advantage by acquiring modern systems or capabilities. The world arms market is willing to provide these advanced systems to countries or individuals with the resources to pay for them. A concerted TECHINT program is vital to providing precise direction and purpose within the US R&D process to ensure that this parity or advantage is neutralized quickly and efficiently.

c.   Examples of Countermeasures. Countermeasures may range from the highly technical, such as reprogramming a frequency in a radar jammer or radar warning receiver, to the analytical changes based on the tactical situation. For example, a TECHINT team or CMEC may determine that the main gun on the primary threat system has a range that is double what was anticipated. Such a determination would force intelligence officers to rethink the disposition of enemy forces and the placement of enemy obstacles and to adjust their analytical products accordingly. This in turn could lead operational planners to rethink objectives, task organizations, and many important operational control measures. In the end, enhanced understanding of enemy capabilities would enable friendly forces to plan and prepare for the warfight in such a way that the enhanced enemy capability would be negated.

3. Scientific and Technical Intelligence Community

a.   The S&TI community satisfies the nation's strategic TECHINT objectives during peacetime and supports operational TECHINT requirements in wartime. The S&TI community starts at the DOD level. Figure I-1 shows this organizational structure.

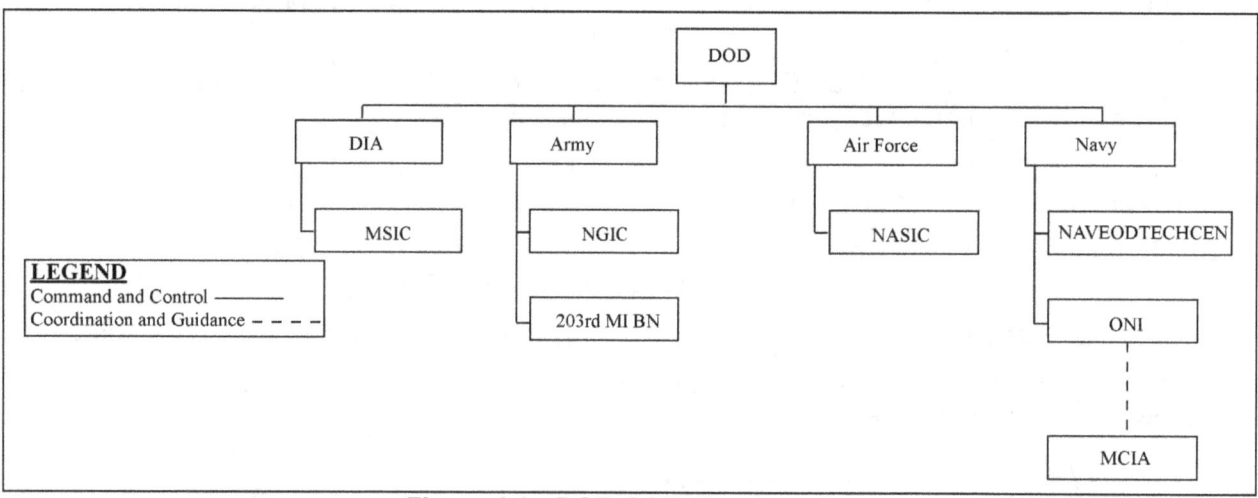

Figure I-1. DOD S&TI Community

b.   S&TI organizations track and analyze foreign technological developments. They analyze the performance and operational capabilities of foreign materiel that may have military application. Although the primary function of the S&TI community is to satisfy strategic TECHINT objectives, it also makes significant contributions toward fulfilling operational and tactical TECHINT requirements. Strategic communications between battlefield TECHINT units and S&TI centers allow the use of their comprehensive databases and expertise to rapidly satisfy the TECHINT requirements of the warfighter.

4. Mission of Battlefield TECHINT

a.   Battlefield TECHINT provides rapid reporting on newly identified foreign weapon system capabilities to combatant commands, joint task forces, and national intelligence centers. Battlefield TECHINT supports operational and planning requirements during wartime operations, worldwide crisis, and contingencies.

b.   Battlefield TECHINT analyzes previously inaccessible and unknown systems to collect rapid intelligence for use by warfighters and collects physical assets for long-term exploitation at national intelligence centers. Classic examples include: The capture of the Wuerzburg Radar during WW II and the identification and exploitation of the Seersucker surface-to-surface (SS) missiles in Desert Storm, the SA-7B in Afghanistan, and the improvised explosive devices in Iraq and Afghanistan. During Operation Restore Hope in Somalia in 1991, TECHINT elements reported a previously misidentified man-portable air defense system (MANPADS) that had much greater capabilities than first thought, resulting in important changes to rotary wing air mission planning and flight rules. These are good examples of how TECHINT enhances force protection during combat and stability and support operation.

c.   Battlefield TECHINT forces perform a unique and highly specialized mission. Their capabilities range from system identification and assessment to sophisticated field exploitation. Their efforts and products contribute to the development of new tactics and countermeasures and their intelligence is used in the development of future US weapon systems.

d.   TECHINT provides rapid reporting on captured enemy materiel (CEM) to commanders. This intelligence supports force protection and the development of new tactics and countermeasures and supports operational decisions based on foreign threats. On occasion, commanders who were unfamiliar with TECHINT capabilities hesitated to employ TECHINT assets and denied them access to vital CEM and facilities. Needless destruction of CEM denied vital intelligence to the warfighter and to national intelligence and security organizations. CEM was also pilfered in the past for the purpose of collecting war trophies. When the TECHINT mission is understood and supported, its assets generate valuable intelligence information for current and future operations. Types of TECHINT missions may include:

- Technical reconnaissance.
- Survey and assessment.
- Technical identification.
- Inventory.
- Sensitive site exploitation (SSE).
- Safety assessment.
- Recovery, packaging, and shipping.
- Field exploitation.
- Battle damage assessment (BDA).
- Prize crew operations (captured vessel operators).

This page intentionally left blank.

Chapter II

ROLES AND RESPONSIBILITIES

1. Introduction

This chapter outlines the various responsibilities of each staff element in units on the battlefield when supporting the overall battlefield TECHINT effort. Battlefield TECHINT elements are resourced and responsible for collecting and processing CEM. Yet to work properly, the battlefield TECHINT structure relies on many other units for mission support, such as combat units which capture items and the transportation units which evacuate items of TECHINT interest.

2. Defense Intelligence Agency (DIA)

DIA, as the primary Joint agency with TECHINT responsibilities, coordinates requirements with theater J-2s and assists during the entire operation plan (OPLAN) development process. Usually, the Service component with the greatest TECHINT interest (e.g., land, or air) will assist DIA during this process. DIA compiles the requirements from the Service intelligence centers and develops the theater specific master requirements list. DIA provides liaison officers and augmentation personnel for the CMEC as required.

3. Service Intelligence Centers

a. Each of the Service intelligence centers provides:

(1) Trained battlefield TECHINT organizations that can deploy on short notice to contingency operations worldwide. Personnel should be equipped with all necessary personal equipment, be qualified on weapons, and possess the technical equipment required for their exploitation operations.

(2) Subject matter experts as required based on exploitation and information requirements.

(3) A theater-specific prioritized list of requirements with sufficient supporting collection information such as photographs, specifications, probable unit associations, etc.

b. Service intelligence centers include:

- Missile and Space Intelligence Center (MSIC)
- National Air and Space Intelligence Center (NASIC)
- National Ground Intelligence Center (NGIC)
- Marine Corps Intelligence Activity (MCIA)
- Office of Naval Intelligence (ONI)
- Armed Forces Medical Intelligence Center (AFMIC)
- Naval Explosive Ordnance Technical Center (NAVEODTECHCEN)

4. 203d Military Intelligence Battalion (203d MI Battalion)

The 203d MI Battalion is the Army's only TECHINT battalion. The mission of the 203d is to deploy worldwide to conduct TECHINT reconnaissance, establish the CMEC, where the CEM is concentrated and exploited at the tactical and operational levels, and to prepare it for shipment to intelligence production centers where it can be exploited at the strategic level. The 203d is also responsible for disseminating the resulting intelligence to combatant commanders and any other relevant parties.

    a.   The 203d MI Battalion conducts TECHINT team collection operations.

    b.   It performs CMEC operations and serves as the base organization of any CMEC when operating in a theater that is considered primarily a land component operation.

    c.   It trains tactical battlefield TECHINT tactics, techniques, and procedures.

    d.   It receives and integrates TECHINT intelligence community augmentation during both team and CMEC operations.

5. Combatant Commanders

    a.   In coordination with DIA, combatant commanders determine what level of TECHINT support is required for mission execution. The basic options for TECHINT support are the employment of a small TECHINT liaison element, one or more TECHINT teams, or establishment of a fully staffed CMEC.

    b.   Combatant commanders inform the National Military Joint Intelligence Center (NMJIC) concerning the level of TECHINT support required.

    c.   The combatant commander's staff, ICW DIA and the lead Service component, develops the TECHINT portion of the OPLAN, and then generates the request for forces (RFF) or request for capability (RFC).

    d.   The combatant commander's staff plans for TECHINT-required facilities, transportation, and communications, and other logistical support.

    e.   Combatant commanders employ TECHINT forces, as required. TECHINT forces should be ready to react to early collection opportunities. TECHINT forces are most effective when employed during decisive operations.

    f.   The J-2 will have the primary responsibility to integrate TECHINT forces in theater, will coordinate collection opportunities, and serves as the combatant commander's principal advisor on TECHINT operations in theater. The J-2 may have liaison officers from DIA that assist with these tasks.

    g.   Combatant commanders provide force protection for TECHINT operations.

6. Other Agencies

    Other agencies may contribute capabilities to the TECHINT mission. These may include the Bureau of Alcohol, Tobacco, Fire arms, and Explosives (ATF), Federal Bureau of Investigation (FBI), Threat Systems Management Office (TSMO), explosive ordnance disposal (EOD) and the Air Force Office of Special Investigations (AFOSI) (see chapter III).

Chapter III

TECHINT UNITS AND CAPABILITIES

1. Department of Defense (DOD) / Joint Organizations

a.   Defense Intelligence Agency (DIA): DIA provides oversight for TECHINT activities throughout DOD during peacetime and war. The S&TI directorate within DIA is the action element for TECHINT. This directorate coordinates with external TECHINT agencies on non-policy matters concerning the production of S&TI.

(1) Defense HUMINT Service (DHS): DHS conducts worldwide HUMINT operations in support of foreign materiel acquisition and exploitation.

(2) Documents Exploitation (DOCEX): DOCEX translates and exploits foreign hard copy and digital media for current relevant information.

b.   Armed Forces Medical Intelligence Center (AFMIC): AFMIC is a DOD intelligence production center under control of DIA. AFMIC is responsible for exploiting foreign medical materiel. The director supports the Army Foreign Materiel Exploitation Program (FMEP) and Army medical R&D requirements.

c.   Missile and Space Intelligence Center (MSIC): MSIC is a DOD intelligence production center under control of DIA and supports the FMEP. The MSIC acquires, produces, maintains, and disseminates S&TI pertaining to missile and space weapons systems, subsystems, components, and activities, such as:

- Antitank guided missiles (ATGMs).
- Tactical air defense.
- Short-range ballistic missiles (SRBMs).
- Directed energy weapons.
- Anti-satellite technology.

d.   Defense Advanced Research Projects Agency (DARPA): The central R&D organization for DOD. It manages and directs selected basic and applied R&D projects for DOD and pursues research and technology where risk and payoff are both very high and where success may provide dramatic advances for traditional military roles and missions. DARPA sponsors R&D in all aspects of TECHINT, imagery intelligence (IMINT), signals intelligence (SIGINT), human intelligence (HUMINT), and measurement and signature intelligence (MASINT).

e.   Defense Threat Reduction Agency (DTRA): DTRA is the DOD agency for counter-proliferation and remediation.

f.   Joint Explosive Ordnance Disposal (EOD) Units: Provide technical intelligence collection and reporting. They provide assessment, identification, disposal, and render safe conventional; chemical, biological, radiological, and nuclear (CBRN); and improvised explosive devices. They also assist in movement, packaging, and hazardous material certification for transportation.

2. Air Force

NASIC is the primary agency producing foreign aerospace S&TI. It satisfies DIA requirements and supports the Air Force Assistant Chief of Staff for Intelligence (AFACSI) by providing subject matter experts (SME) and TECHINT collection teams for deployable capability. NASIC acquires, analyzes, produces, and disseminates information related to current and future enemy aerospace capabilities including:

- Aircraft, air-launched weapons systems and munitions, electronic attack, communication systems, unmanned aerial vehicles, and radar systems.

- Ground-based systems including ground control intercept radars, target acquisition radars associated with surface-to-air missile (SAM) complexes; air defense command, control, and communications (C3) systems; and camouflage, concealment, and deception (CC&D) equipment such as paints, nets, and target decoys.

3. Army

a. Office of the Deputy Chief of Staff, Intelligence (ODCSINT): Although ODCSINT does not produce intelligence; it does have general staff responsibility for all Army TECHINT activities. The ODCSINT:

- Formulates policies and procedures for S&TI activities.

- Supervises and carries out the Army S&TI program.

- Coordinates Department of the Army (DA) staff and major subordinate command requirements for TECHINT.

- Is responsible for the Army Foreign Materiel Program (FMP).

b. 20th Support Command (chemical, biological radioactive, nuclear, or high yield explosives [CBRNE]): The 20th Support Command integrates, coordinates, deploys, and provides trained and ready forces and is prepared to exercise command and control of full-spectrum CBRNE operations to joint and Army force commanders. The command maintains technical links with appropriate joint, federal, and state CBRNE assets, as well as research, development, and technical communities to assure Army CBRNE response readiness. The organization also provides training and readiness oversight to the 111th Ordnance Group (EOD). As requested, they provide technical expertise and assistance to the continental US Armies in support of the training and readiness oversight of reserve component CBRNE forces.

(1) 52nd Ordnance Group/111th Ordnance Group (EOD): These units deploy trained EOD forces and exercise command and control of EOD operations to support combatant commanders and military installations. They provide military support/assistance to civil authorities to detect, identify, render safe, and dispose of unexploded ordnance and improvised explosive devices. Additionally, they react to chemical, biological, radiological, and nuclear (CBRN) explosive incidents which threaten forces, citizens, or operations in or outside the continental United States. Upon request, they provide EOD support to the US Secret Service and the US State Department. They transform the EOD program to meet future requirements.

(2) Technical Escort (TE) Battalion: A TE battalion is charged with identification, assessment, render safe, movement, and remediation of foreign and domestic chemical and biological munitions, devices, and hazardous materials.

c. US Army Intelligence and Security Command (INSCOM):

(1) Under the direction of Headquarters, Department of the Army (HQDA), INSCOM is a major Army command and is responsible for peacetime TECHINT operations. Headquarters, INSCOM, fulfills its responsibilities through its TECHINT oversight function and manages the Army's Foreign Materiel for Training (FMT) Program and FMEP. It does this by:

(a) Providing the interface with strategic S&TI agencies in support of foreign materiel exploitation.

(b) Organizing, training, and equipping echelons above corps (EAC) TECHINT organizations during peacetime.

(2) Headquarters, INSCOM is the parent organization of NGIC and manages the Army's Foreign Materiel Program (FMP). NGIC produces and maintains intelligence on foreign scientific developments, ground force weapons systems, and associated technologies. NGIC analysis includes, but is not limited to, military comm-electronics (C-E) systems including:

(a) Types of aircraft used by foreign ground forces (usually rotary wing).

(b) CBRN systems.

(c) Basic research in civilian technologies with possible military applications.

(3) INSCOM further provides the Active Component (AC) personnel and resource contribution to the Military Intelligence Readiness Command's (MIRC) 203d MI Battalion.

d. Military Intelligence Readiness Command (MIRC):

(1) MIRC is the US Army Reserve Command's (USARC) functional command charged with providing command and control of Army Reserve military intelligence units and Soldiers.

(2) MIRC is the parent organization of the 203d MI Battalion. The 203d MI BN is headquartered at Aberdeen Proving Ground, MD, and is the Army's only TECHINT battalion. The 203d MI BN:

- Conducts TECHINT reporting and collection in support of validated operational and standing S&TI objectives.

- Acts as the HQDA executive agent for foreign materiel used for training purposes.

- Conducts formalized operational TECHINT training for DOD analysts and for both AC and Reserve Component (RC) TECHINT personnel.

- Supports NGIC's foreign materiel acquisition (FMA) operations and foreign materiel exploitation (FME) operations as directed.

- Forms core element of CMEC in support of ground combat operations. Provides logistics and infrastructure to absorb joint and interagency TECHINT assets in order to form CMEC.

- Provides the capability to field/deploy TECHINT collection teams and conducts warehousing, in-country exploitation, packaging, and CEM transportation operations. Also conducts collection management and dissemination (CM&D) of CEM.

- Provides military TECHINT analysts, who work with remotely located SMEs on ground-based weapons systems, munitions, vehicles, and communications systems.

- Responds to emerging TECHINT missions associated with counterinsurgency operations. Forms weapons intelligence teams (WIT) to conduct forensic analysis in support of EOD operations. The WITs are task organized to operate with EOD forces and provide a direct link between EOD companies and brigade combat teams.

e. US Army Materiel Command (AMC): AMC is a major Army command with a significant support role in TECHINT. Among AMC elements are a series of research, development, and engineering centers (ARDECs), the Army Research Laboratory System, and the US Army Test and Evaluation Command (TECOM). Each element plays a role in wartime in conducting highly technical evaluations of foreign equipment. In peacetime, the AMC conducts FME on equipment purchased by each laboratory and by the research, development, and engineering center (RDEC) for the intelligence community and for DOD as part of the International Materiel Evaluation Program (IMEP). AMC's foreign ordnance exploitation team is at the Fire Support Armaments Center (FSAC) EOD (Picatinny Arsenal). They exploit foreign ground ordnance and develop render safe procedures (RSP) for foreign ordnance. They also prepare detailed intelligence reports to support EOD, intelligence, and US munitions developer communities.

4. Navy

a.   The Navy proponent for TECHINT in the ONI is designated ONI-23. ONI provides S&TI on technical characteristics and capabilities of foreign naval forces and merchant systems and manages the Navy's Foreign Materiel Program (FMP). It provides S&TI support to the commander of the ONI and the Chief of Naval Operations. ONI:

- Provides SMEs in sea-based weapon systems, weapons, munitions, platforms, merchant vessels, and communication systems.

- Provides capability to field/deploy TECHINT collection teams, in-country exploitation, and packaging of CEM.

b.   NAVEODTECHCEN is the training center for all joint EOD personnel. It acts as the primary center for establishing identification, RSP, and demolition procedures for foreign ordnance. It is augmented by Army EOD specialists from Picatinny Arsenal.

c.   NAVEOD Scientific and Technical Intelligence Liaison Officer (STILO): The STILO expedites initial reporting and coordinates CMEC efforts by embedding TECHINT personnel with corps and equivalent units. The STILO is responsible for examining CEM in the field and reports findings to the supported commander. The STILO also provides advice on handling, control, and evacuation procedures of CEM. Through coordination with the STILO, Corps and equivalent units transport or arrange for the movement of selected items to the CMEC. The STILO is attached to each Corps or appropriate subordinate command as directed by the theater commander.

5. Other Agencies

Other agencies with potential TECHINT involvement that may provide personnel, equipment, and expertise to a CMEC include:

- National Security Agency (NSA)

- Central Intelligence Agency (CIA)

- Federal Bureau of Investigation (FBI)

- Bureau of Alcohol, Tobacco, Fire Arms and Explosives (ATF)

- Department of Energy (DOE)

- Department of State (DOS)

- Combined Explosive Exploitation Cell (CEXC)

- Chemical Materials Agency (CMA)

- Research, Development, and Engineering Command (RDECOM)

- Joint Chemical, Biological, Radiological, and Nuclear Defense (JCBRND)

- Soldiers System Center (SSC)

Chapter IV

TECHINT TEAM OPERATIONS

1. Introduction

This chapter describes battlefield TECHINT operations, functions, and procedures. Battlefield TECHINT operations consist of planning, collection, field exploitation, initial TECHINT reporting, analysis, evacuation (as necessary), detailed exploitation and analysis, and production and dissemination of final TECHINT products. The term "battlefield" includes any area of operation that US forces occupy while conducting the full range of military operations.

a. Battlefield TECHINT can start with identifying something new, modified, or unexpected in the order of battle within the area of operations and taking the proper steps to report it.

b. The information or item is initially exploited to ascertain if it represents an advantage for the enemy or presents a technical surprise for friendly forces. If it does, the information or item then undergoes increasing levels of analysis until a countermeasure or TTP is developed and the technological advantage is neutralized. While a single weapon or technology seldom means the difference between final victory and defeat, it can give one side a battlefield advantage.

c. Battlefield TECHINT is an intelligence mission assigned to the joint force commander's (JFC) J-2. When a CMEC is established, it is aligned under the J-2. The JTF Commander determines the joint CMEC (JCMEC) command relationships.

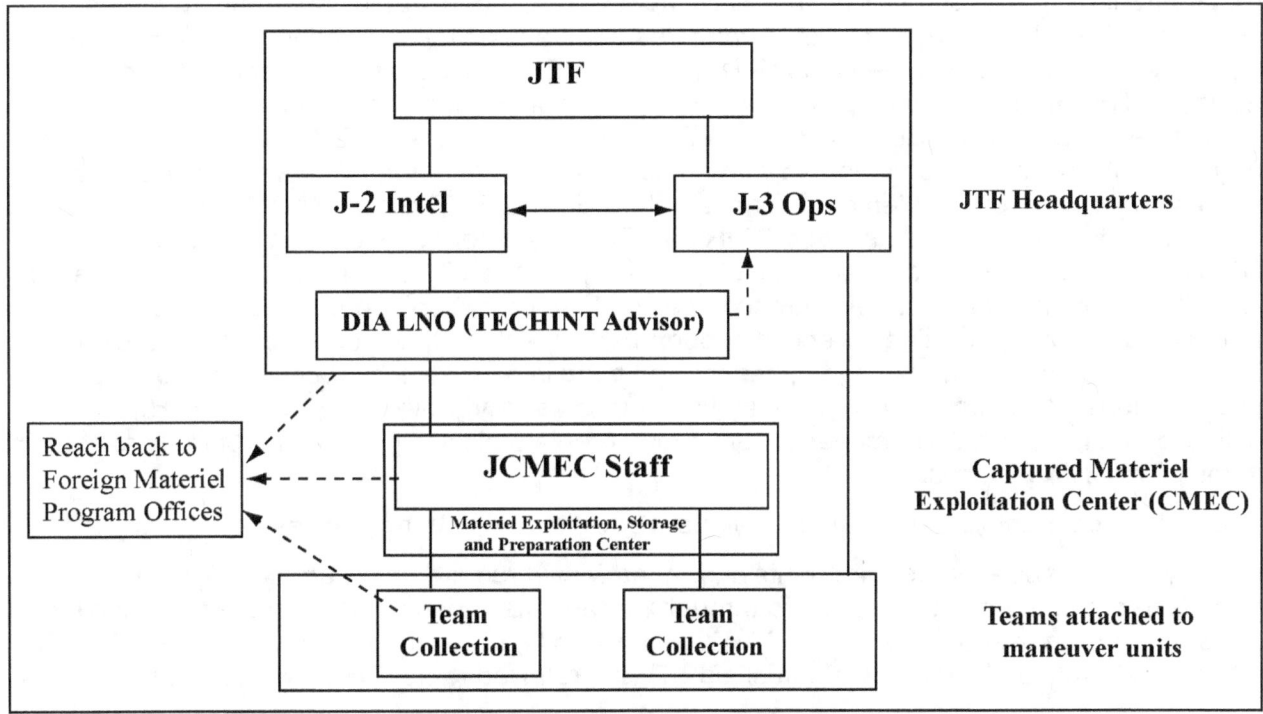

Figure IV-1. JTF Information Flow

2. Task Organization, Tasking, and Employment of TECHINT

a. TECHINT assets are task organized based on theater/national intelligence requirements, tactical and theater force structure, threat environment, and assigned mission and role.

b.   TECHINT assets and other assets assigned to a TECHINT effort may consist of multi-Service and intra-agency components such as military tactical intelligence battalions, in-country exploitation teams (ICE), STILO from Naval Intelligence, Air Force foreign materiel exploitation teams, EOD teams, technical escort (TE) units, DIA, CIA, ATF, FBI, DOE, DTRA, DHS, Department of Health (DH), NSA, national laboratories, and others to include functional assets such as document exploitation (DOCEX), chemical and biological intelligence support team (CBIST), medical exploitation (MEDEX), HUMINT, hazardous material transportation office (HMTO), Combined Explosive Exploitation Cell (CEXC), and weapons intelligence teams (WIT). Assets also include assigned or attached security and logistic support elements.

c.   In many operations the involvement of coalition (non-US) partners has become the standard. This has also been true in recent TECHINT operations. Multi-national (coalition) operations require special planning for command and control (C2), intelligence sharing, communications, and combat service support (CSS) requirements. The OPLAN or a fragmentary order (FRAG order) can be used to establish these relationships.

3. TECHINT Operations Cycle

a.   Intelligence Preparation of the Battlespace (IPB): Once the combatant commander has determined the priority intelligence requirements (PIRs) and intelligence requirements (IRs), the assigned TECHINT planner analyzes those requirements to determine where and how TECHINT may provide information to help answer them. Given national requirements for S&TI, the assigned TECHINT planner may recommend inclusion of several TECHINT intelligence requirements to the existing PIRs and IRs. The assigned TECHINT planner and staff then develop technical intelligence taskings and roles and develop the commander's TECHINT PIR, IR, and specific information requests (SIR) for the CMEC and TECHINT collection teams. The assigned TECHINT planner helps develop TECHINT commander's critical information requirements (CCIR) and SIR of a TECHINT nature. The assigned TECHINT planner ensures requirements are closely coordinated with combatant command J-2, or theater Army G-2, as well as major subordinate elements: for example, Corps G-2. The assigned TECHINT planner then integrates and deconflicts these CCIR and SIR with other items of special interest to the S&TI community in conjunction with developing the prioritized TECHINT requirements collection list. The requirements list should be accompanied by a collection support package to support targeting and collection. The collection support package should include probable or expected locations, photographs and imagery, hazard and handling instructions, and other known specifications. The format of this list may vary, but is usually provided by DIA. TECHINT collection teams attached to maneuver units may preplan missions to sites most likely to contain items of TECHINT interest.

b.   Requirements Dissemination to Maneuver Units and Other Agencies:

(1)   National-level requirements and theater-level requirements are consolidated and prioritized at the J-2 and disseminated through military intelligence and operations channels by the all-source analysis element. The CMEC templates likely locations where items of TECHINT interest will likely be found on the battlefield. This is referred to as "TECHINT templating."

(2) The TECHINT collection list is normally found in the TECHINT appendix to the Intelligence Annex to the operations order (OPORD) at all echelons above maneuver brigade or group. Appropriate units are notified, through intelligence channels that these items may be within their areas of operations and are tasked for collection through operational channels. The taskings must be translated into terms that combat, support, and specific collectors can understand. TECHINT personnel communicate TECHINT requirements using an appropriate presentation format.

c.   Equipment Capture, Notification, and Intelligence Value Assessment (Capture Notification Reporting). When maneuver units capture materiel identified on the collection requirements list or come across materiel that remains unidentified, appears modified, or is otherwise out of the ordinary or unexpected, a size, activity, location, unit/uniform, time, and equipment (SALUTE) report must be generated and sent back through reporting channels. Units should strive to safeguard materiel or transport to safe holding areas if the security environment permits, but only if materiel is safe for transport/storage as determined by EOD. If materiel must be destroyed or left in place, all efforts to obtain photos of items, grid coordinates, and factory markings/serial numbers should be taken. Documents associated with captured equipment should be collected and sent through intelligence channels to the CMEC, where they will be processed prior to shipment into DOCEX channels. Equipment should be tagged by the capturing units as indicated in appendix E (Marking and Tagging).

(1) The TECHINT LNO at corps G-2 (or lowest level) monitors reporting for information relating to materiel of technical intelligence value. A designated member of the J-2 serves as the primary LNO between the CMEC, DIA, the Service centers, and the JTF. The LNOs screen reports arriving from intelligence reporting channels.

(2) The TECHINT LNO compares reporting information with outstanding requirements to see if collection is necessary. Depending on the priority of the requirement and tactical situation, the TECHINT LNO will:

- Coordinate with the G-3 to transport and task the corps TECHINT collection team to the capture site.

- Give further instructions for exploitation and/or evacuation procedures to the capturing unit S-2.

(3) If an intelligence requirement no longer exists for the captured equipment, the TECHINT LNO informs the capturing S-2 and coordinates the disposal of the materiel within normal logistics channels.

(4) The corps TECHINT LNO forwards an information copy of the SALUTE report, with details of initial actions taken, to the CMEC and TECHINT teams.

(5) The TECHINT teams reach back to the CMEC or the Service intelligence centers to obtain SME assessment of the captured materiel and their recommended disposition (detailed in-country exploitation, component recovery, retrograde, or destruction).

d.   Mission Planning and Approval (FRAGOrder): Upon notification of equipment capture, a TECHINT team and their supporting security support element must plan and gain approval for the TECHINT mission to the site. A TECHINT team must be identified and notified for mission execution. The team should be task organized for a specific mission, with the right type of expertise and equipment. The mission commander should normally be the individual best able to lead the TECHINT team to successfully obtain raw battlefield intelligence that satisfies the commander's PIRs and CCIRs. This mission commander selection should be situation and individual dependent. Other support requirements must be tasked and included for the mission as required, such as logistics, support, and appropriate transportation assets. Route planning, unit to unit coordination, communications, and checkpoints are the responsibility of the mission commander. Overall mission plans should cover the items in the mission planning checklist in appendix C (Checklists).

e.   TECHINT Exploitation Mission Execution Phases:

(1) Tactical movement is led by, or is executed in coordination with, the security element providing support to TECHINT.

(2) Securing the site is also the responsibility of the security support element or the unit in control of the site to be exploited.

(3) EOD should ensure area is safe to conduct exploitation operations and hazardous materials/weapons/weapon systems are in a condition supportive of exploitation plan.

(4) Once a TECHINT unit takes custody of a TECHINT item, battlefield TECHINT exploitation begins. TECHINT analysts and specialists use checklists and standard operating procedures (SOPs) established by S&TI agencies and the CMEC to exploit each type of threat equipment for which requirements exist. Disposition requirements for CEM must be assessed during the technical exploitation process.

(5) Marking and tagging CEM should be accomplished by TECHINT teams in accordance with appendix E (Marking and Tagging).

(6) Teams coordinate disposition of assets. For items assessed to require further exploitation, TECHINT teams prepare CEM for transportation and coordinate the movement in accordance with the procedures in appendix F (Movement and Storage of Captured Materiel). Disposition may include destruction, limited exploitation, disablement, or complete/partial transport. Tactical movement back to base is executed in coordination with the security element providing support to TECHINT

f. TECHINT Reporting:

(1) The TECHINT team is responsible for producing the preliminary technical report (PRETECHREP) (see appendix B) on all materiel exploited within 24 hours of discovery via what ever appropriately classification communications that are available.

(2) A complementary technical intelligence report (COMTECHREP) (see appendix B) may be required when CEM assessed the asset to have intelligence value or when directed by J-2 or CMEC. Service intelligence centers may request COMTECHREP reporting.

(3) TECHINT reporting from CMEC or TECHINT teams to the theater Analysis and Control Element (ACE) is conducted through existing communications channels.

(4) The CMEC sends its completed products to the J-2 and to the theater ACE. This report is based on the standard intelligence information report (IIR) format. TECHINT reports are then disseminated through two channels. The ACE fuses the TECHINT single-source product into its all-source reports and disseminates them through normal intelligence channels. While the TECHINT single-source product is being integrated into the ACE all-source product, the CMEC disseminates the single-source TECHINT product through TECHINT communications channels to the national S&TI centers in the continental United States (CONUS). This ensures both the rapid dissemination of TECHINT and the fusion of TECHINT into all-source products. The CMEC ensures that reports to include exploitation results are disseminated within theater.

4. TECHINT Support to Sensitive Site Exploitation

Task organized TECHINT teams are assigned to support the exploitation of sensitive sites identified through pre-combat intelligence or daily reporting from maneuver forces. The site may, or may not, have significant CEM value, however, the identified site should be of critical value to the combatant commander and must be fully exploited for all intelligence value. Sensitive sites may include research and design laboratories, factories, depots, seaports, airfields, headquarters, and scientific facilities.

Chapter V

CAPTURED MATERIEL EXPLOITATION CENTER (CMEC)

1. Captured Materiel Exploitation Center (CMEC)

a. When established by the JTF combatant commander, CMEC conducts TECHINT operations against enemy air, sea, and ground forces in combat and contingency operations and participates in related peacetime training activities such as exercises and war games where technical intelligence applies.

b. The recovery of CEM is both a combatant command and national requirement. Subsequent exploitation of CEM can provide critical intelligence on enemy strengths and weaknesses that can favorably influence operational planning and force protection. The CMEC normally conducts this exploitation mission. Combatant commands or subordinate joint forces should notify the National Military Joint Intelligence Center (NMJIC) through command channels that CMEC support is required. This will ensure that appropriate Service component resources are allocated.

c. TECHINT is the process of identification, assessment, collection, exploitation, and evacuation of CEM in support of national technical intelligence requirements. TECHINT acquired through CMEC operations provides rapid performance and vulnerability assessments of enemy equipment, giving a critical edge to US forces in current and future operations.

d. Each Service has dedicated TECHINT organizations capable of supporting CMEC operations. These organizations receive specialized training to effectively operate in hostile and austere environments.

e. The process for tasking and employing TECHINT operations in the joint environment begins at the unified command level. Each unified command must have a designated TECHINT planner within the intelligence directorate to coordinate requirements with national intelligence production centers and the joint staff.

f. TECHINT is an intelligence mission assigned to the J-2, who is responsible for CMEC activities. The CMEC executes mission assignments based on national collection requirement priorities. The J-2 coordinates support for CMEC missions with DIA. The CMEC commander reports directly to the J-2 to integrate new technical intelligence into current joint force intelligence reports.

2. Role and Mission of DIA LNOs (Technical Advisors)

a. The DIA technical advisor is the primary J-2 staff element with TECHINT responsibility and serves as the requirements control authority for the CMEC. The advisor deploys upon notification by the theater commander when TECHINT operations will be conducted in a theater of operations.

b. DIA technical advisors provide the proper coordination necessary for the maximum effective collection, exploitation, extraction, and assessment of CEM. DIA advisors provide TECHINT advice and assistance to the theater J-2. They also act as the TECHINT collection LNO for the theater. They coordinate with national exploitation organizations and provide a CEM priority list to J-2. They coordinate closely with DIA to ensure both national and theater level foreign materiel collection requirements are satisfied.

3. Role and Mission of the Captured Materiel Exploitation Center (CMEC)

a.   The CMEC acts as the central location for the collection, safeguarding, identification, battlefield exploitation and reporting, and evacuation of CEM that has intelligence value.

b.   The theater commander determines the location of the CMEC. This location facilitates the storage, movement, and evacuation of CEM. The CMEC must consider force protection requirements and have easy access to communications, transportation, and other support facilities. The CMEC should be located in close proximity to the Joint Document Exploitation Center (JDEC), the Joint Interrogation and Debriefing Center (JIDC), and the Captured Ammunition Holding Area (CAHA). The CMEC, JDEC, and JIDC facilities have common site selection criteria and complimentary functions that provide efficient allocation of assets for movement, safeguarding, exploitation, and evacuation of captured enemy personnel, equipment, and materiel.

c.   The CMEC functions as the theater's central CEM and materiel exploitation facility. As such it:

(1) Establishes procedures for the exploitation and evacuation of CEM in coordination with the J-4.

(2) Produces and disseminates tactical intelligence reports and preliminary technical reports.

(3) Monitors the collection of priority CEM upon notification.

(4) Secures and maintains an inventory of all CEM.

(5) Assists in the processing and shipping of CEM from theater for further analysis and exploitation.

(6) Operates with personnel assembled from Service TECHINT assets and capabilities. The theater commander supports CMEC operations with augmenting security forces, explosive ordnance disposal personnel, transportation elements, and other "base-level" activities as needed. The CMEC commander and deputy are appointed by DIA and are responsible for the overall operation and administration of the CMEC. Upon notification that a CMEC is required in theater, normally it will consist of the following sections:

(a) Operations Center. The operations center is responsible for the planning and coordination of all current and projected CMEC operations including the deployment of STILOs and TECHINT collection teams. The operations center maintains the current CEM intelligence situation.

(b) Support Center. The support center is responsible for providing administrative and logistics support to all CMEC elements and personnel.

(c) Storage Center. The storage center maintains all records on CEM that is processed through or by the CMEC. This includes any structure and/or facility that has been inspected or reviewed by CMEC personnel.

(d) Communications Center. The communications center is responsible for providing communications, automated information systems, and related maintenance support to all CMEC elements.

(e) Exploitation Center. The exploitation center processes validated requirements, exploits CEM, produces intelligence reports, and ensures dissemination of TECHINT data.

(f) Scientific and Technical Intelligence Liaison Officers (STILOs). The STILO expedites initial reporting and coordinates CMEC efforts by embedding TECHINT personnel with corps and equivalent units. The STILO is responsible for examining CEM in the field and reports findings to the supported commander. The STILO also provides advice on handling, control, and evacuation procedures of CEM. Through coordination with the STILO, corps and equivalent units transport or arrange for the movement of selected items to the CMEC. The STILO is attached to each corps or appropriate subordinate command as directed by the theater commander.

4. Responsibilities

    a.   Chairman of the Joint Chiefs of Staff (CJCS)

        (1) Identify and include, in all applicable implementing orders, TECHINT mission objectives, priorities, and taskings.

        (2) Plan for and coordinate the deployment of TECHINT forces with the combatant commands and the Military Departments.

        (3) Promulgate joint TECHINT doctrine.

        (4) Establish a position on the Joint Staff to coordinate integration of TECHINT forces into operations and identify requirements for the Joint Staff. The incumbent of this position shall be the CJCS representative on the Joint TECHINT Planning Group (JTIPG).

    b.   Combatant Commanders

        (1) Plan for, task, deploy, and employ TECHINT forces during wartime operations, contingencies, joint exercises, and other events involving CEM of intelligence value. In all applicable crisis and deliberate plans, include a TECHINT appendix that establishes a joint TECHINT concept of operations and the initial collection requirements.

        (2) Assist TECHINT forces in coordinating facilities, transportation, and communications and provide other logistical support to sustain deployed personnel.

        (3) Plan to employ TECHINT forces during the initial phase of an operation to ensure TECHINT collection on critical CEM.

        (4) Identify a TECHINT staff position within the J-2 to plan for the employment of TECHINT forces. The TECHINT staff position will have the primary responsibility to integrate TECHINT forces in theater and coordinate collection opportunities. The incumbent of this position is the combatant command representative in the JTIPG.

        (5) Ensure tasking and requests for forces, identify the operational controlling authority for TECHINT forces, and provide an in-theater point of contact for initial coordination.

        (6) Ensure TECHINT data is reviewed for protection of classified information and transmitted in accordance with applicable security regulations and local instructions.

        (7) Coordinate with the Joint Staff to publish specific guidelines for exploitation data distribution, clearance, and security classification requirements.

        (8) Include within Command, Control and Communication Systems Annex of the operations plan the communication requirements necessary for the transmission of TECHINT data to DIA and national intelligence centers.

    c.   Service Components

        (1) Air Force

            (a) Headquarters United States Air Force

- Establish Air Force TECHINT doctrine.

- Designate an O-6 or civilian equivalent representative to the JTIPG.

- Notify the Air Intelligence Agency (AIA) and appropriate major commands, with HQ USAF/TE coordination, of any short-term, time-sensitive collection requirements.

- Monitor TECHINT activities.

- Provide TECHINT collection and exploitation teams as tasked.

(b) Air Intelligence Agency

- Provide overall policy and guidance for TECHINT functions and associated capabilities.

- Appoint a TECHINT functional manager as the AIA focal point for TECHINT operations.

- Program and budget for resources to sustain TECHINT functions.

- Coordinate with DIA on CMEC participation.

- Provide TECHINT collection and exploitation teams as tasked.

(c) National Air and Space Intelligence Center

- Provide prioritized exploitation requirements for Air Force TECHINT operations.

- Establish a training program to ensure Air Force TECHINT teams can accomplish TECHINT requirements.

- Assume primary responsibility for Air Force TECHINT functions.

- Provide TECHINT collection and exploitation teams as tasked.

- Provide CMEC support staff as required.

- Provide STILOs as required.

(2) Army

(a) Provide TECHINT organizations (LNO to battalion) for team operations and CMEC establishment.

(b) Provide supporting TECHINT staff for OPLAN development.

(c) Serve as lead organization for TTP in land operations.

(d) Provide rotational sustainment for prolonged operations.

(e) Mobilize and deploy RC TECHINT units for early utilization during decisive maneuver phase if applicable.

(f) Receive and integrate joint augmentation (military and civilian) into the CMEC structure.

(g) Provide security, EOD, communications, and dedicated transportation assets as required for CMEC operations.

(3) Navy

(a) Chief of Naval Operations. Provide overall policy and guidance for TECHINT functions and associated capabilities (OPNAVINST 3882.2A).

(b) Director of Naval Intelligence (DNI). Appoint a functional manager as the Navy focal point for TECHINT operations.

(c) Office of Naval Intelligence

- Coordinate with DIA on CMEC operations.

- Designate a representative to the JTIPG.

- Provide prioritized exploitation requirements for Navy TECHINT operations.

- Establish a training program to ensure Navy/Navy Reserve TECHINT teams can accomplish TECHINT requirements.

- Assume primary responsibility for Navy TECHINT functions.

- Provide TECHINT ICE teams as tasked.

5. Resource Requirements

a. DIA is responsible for special requirements for CMEC operations (in regards to transportation assets, communications assets, and the full range of logistics support).

b. Services are responsible for training personnel and providing individual equipment for mission responsibilities. Services are also responsible for providing specialized TECHINT equipment necessary to meet mission requirements.

6. CMEC Concept of Operations

The CMEC and TECHINT teams produce technical intelligence reports and other products which are transmitted to the J-2 and to other locations via portable and fixed long-range transmission systems, such as satellite communication (SATCOM), Non-secure Internet Protocol Router Network (NIPRNET), SECRET Internet Protocol Router Network (SIPRNET), etc. The following procedures are applicable to every CMEC deployment:

a. Identification. Maneuver units identify and report suspected items of intelligence value via SALUTE report. TECHINT teams may be dispatched to confirm identification of items reported thru maneuver units. TECHINT teams will also execute preplanned missions to strategic facilities and locations to identify items on the master requirements list.

b. Assessment. Once items have been identified, CMEC assess the CEM to determine its overall intelligence value. System upgrades and modifications are analyzed to determine if further exploitation is required.

c. Collection. CMEC personnel will inventory all identified items of interest. Items determined to be of intelligence value will be transported either to the CAHA or CMEC. Munitions will be marked for transportation to a CAHA and all other items will be marked for transport to the CMEC. All items of interest will undergo limited in-place exploitation.

d. Exploitation. Exploitation efforts seek to determine technical properties of CEM. The resultant exploitation reports are disseminated to the theater staff, DIA, and to appropriate national intelligence production center dissemination.

e. Transmission and Distribution. TECHINT data is moved through the CMEC to national intelligence centers within 24-48 hours to meet S&TI requirements. Figure V-1 depicts TECHINT data flow from CMEC teams to national intelligence centers. CMEC teams can deploy with limited stand-alone transmission capability via man-portable low data-rate satellite transmission systems. Most TECHINT data is moved using theater-deployed communications or fixed communications, such as NIPRNET and SIPRNET.

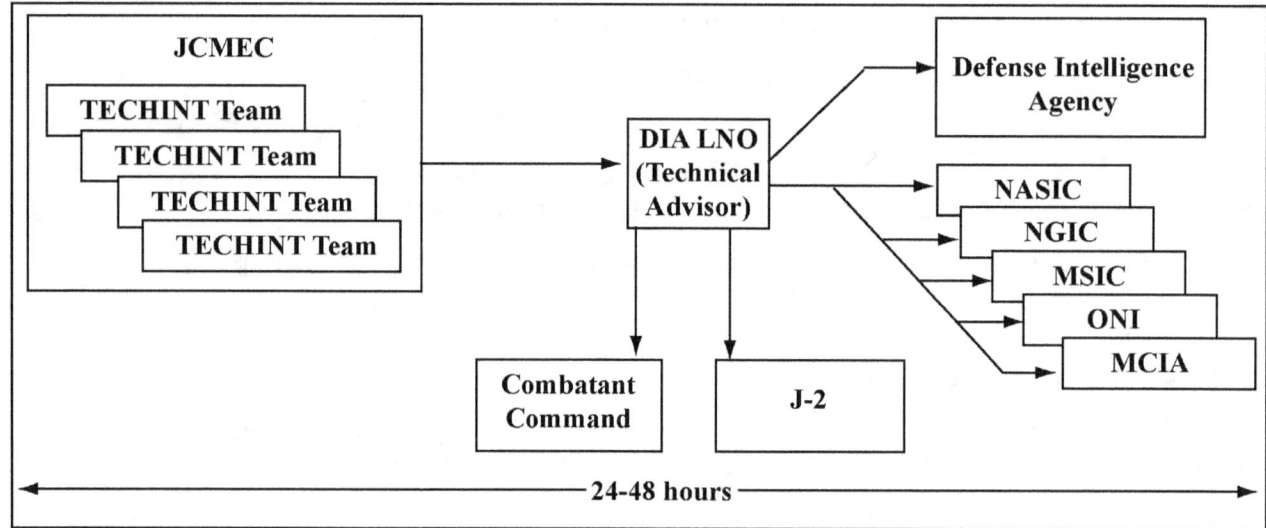

Figure V-1. TECHINT Data Flow

f. Evacuation. Evacuation of CEM is based on priorities established in the master requirements list.

7. Forms Prescribed/Adopted

The form in this publication is adopted. For form designation and title, see table of contents under figure E-1.

Appendix A

SAMPLE TECHINT APPENDIX TO AN INTELLIGENCE ANNEX

This appendix contains the example provided in FM 34-54, *Technical Intelligence*, 30 January 1998, Appendix D, and is extracted in its entirety.

This appendix provides examples of TECHINT input to an intelligence annex and TECHINT-related tabs to that annex. The TECHINT appendix is used—

- As the primary example for the J-4/G-4 appendix on captured weapons.

- As the example for the J-1/G-1 appendix on equipment taken from EPWs.

THEATER ARMY INTELLIGENCE ANNEX

This example is tailored for a theater Army headquarters. All headquarters, however, should include TECHINT operations input.

1. **SUMMARY OF ENEMY SITUATION.**

2. **INTELLIGENCE REQUIREMENTS.**

    a. PIR:

        (1) Does the enemy have significant quantities of night vision devices?

        (2) Is there unusual or unexplained damage to US equipment and materiel?

        (3) Have there been unexpected defensive and/or offensive capabilities of enemy equipment?

    b. IR: What are the capabilities and/or limitations of the AT-5 ATGM?

3. **INTELLIGENCE ACQUISITION TASKS.**

    a. General: Capture of any enemy materiel will be immediately reported through intelligence channels in accordance with priorities described below.

        (1) 15th Corps. Priority of collection on foreign equipment is T-64B, AT-5, and SA-13.

        (2) 25th Corps. Priority of collection on foreign equipment is BTR-70, BMP-I, and individual protective vest (body armor).

        (3) 23d MI Brigade (EAC).

            (a) 1st Battalion.

            (b) 2d Battalion.

            (c) 3d Battalion.

    b. One TECHINT collection team and TECHINT liaison team to operate within each corps area attached to each corps MI brigade.

c.   Screening and exploitation of captured IEW priorities described in FM 34-54, Appendix B.

d.   Fully integrate TECHINT operations and teams with IEW and EPW operations.

4. MEASURES FOR HANDLING PERSONNEL, DOCUMENTS, AND MATERIEL.

a.   Personnel.

b.   Documents.

c.   Materiel.

(1) All materiel will be reported in accordance with procedures and priorities described in Appendix XXX, TECHINT.

(2) All materiel will be evacuated to the nearest collection point and held for TECHINT screening in accordance with Appendix XXX, TECHINT.

(3) Items designated by TECHINT personnel as possessing intelligence value will be evacuated to destinations designated by TECHINT personnel in accordance with priorities described in Appendix XXX, TECHINT.

(4) No materiel will be diverted for other uses until screened and released by TECHINT personnel.

5. REPORTS AND DISTRIBUTION. All equipment-related intelligence, SALUTE, and EPW reports will include the J-2/G-2 and CMEC as an addressee.

JOINT THEATER TECHNICAL INTELLIGENCE APPENDIX

This is an example of a joint theater TECHINT appendix. It shows how CEM must be handled, reported, and its disposition.

Appendix XX, TECHINT, to Annex, Intelligence, to OPLAN/OPORD.

[This example does not include the tabs that are referenced and listed at the end.]

REFERENCES:

a.   OPLAN _____

b.   FM 34-54.

c.   FM 3-19-1.

d.   Chemical and Biological Sampling, Transport, and Evaluation Management Procedures, dated February 1986.

1. PURPOSE: This appendix establishes policy and prescribes responsibilities and procedures for the proper handling, reporting, intelligence assessment, and disposition of CEM. Additionally, it establishes the procedures for the safe and expedient collection of suspected CB agents to the laboratory for processing, analysis, and identification.

2. POLICY:

a.   The J-2 controls and directs the theater captured materiel exploitation program. The CMEC within the J-2 carries out exploitation activities.

b.   The CMEC will be formed from elements of the 203d MI Battalion (TECHINT), _____ MI Brigade.

c.   The _____ J-2 exercises staff responsibility over the intelligence exploitation of CEM throughout the area of operations and establishes requirements for evacuation of specific items to CONUS for further exploitation. An LNE from the CMEC will be located in the J-2.

d.   Commander, 203d MI Battalion (TECHINT):

(1) Establishes the CMEC and attaches a TECHINT team to each Corps; positions an LNE with the J-2, each Corps G-2, the theater MI Brigade, and theater interrogation.

(2) In coordination with the Theater/Army Surgeon General, advises the J-2/G-2 on all matters of CB sampling.

(3) Recommends a theater souvenir and war trophy policy in accordance with FM 34-54, Appendix C.

e.   The J-3:

(1) In coordination with the J-2, approves requests and assigns priorities for the issue of CEM to US units engaged in special missions or training based on the following prioritized uses of captured materiel:

(a)   Intelligence.

(b)   Special warfare.

(c)   Special operation forces.

(d)   Issue to friendly forces.

(e)   Internal defense.

(f)   Substitutes or supplements to US equipment.

(g)   Distribution to friendly foreign units or groups.

(2) Coordinates provisions of EOD support as required in the exploitation of CEM in accordance with AR 75-15 and to fill requirements stated by the J-2.

(a)   The J-4 exercises staff supervision over the evacuation and movement of CEM of intelligence value in the theater to the CMEC and coordinates evacuation of high priority items back to CONUS.

(b)   The Staff Judge Advocate provides legal guidance concerning the disposition of certain categories of enemy materiel, structures, and facilities.

(c)   See Tab D of this appendix for CB sampling responsibilities.

3. RESPONSIBILITIES:

a.   The CMEC is charged with the conduct and coordination of assessment of CEM within the command. Support in the assessment of enemy naval and aerodynamic systems and materiel will be provided by intelligence personnel from the Navy and Air Force components attached to the CMEC. The scope of responsibilities include:

(1) Assign an LNE to the J-2, G-2, and the theater interrogation facility.

(2) Deploy TECHINT collection teams forward to each deployed Corps to conduct preliminary screening of evacuated materiel and to respond to targets of opportunity which cannot be processed in a normal manner.

(3) Receive/process validated intelligence requirements for items of enemy materiel.

(4) Participate in the technical interrogation of EPWs and assist in screening CEDs.

(5) Examine and evaluate TECHINT reporting and classification of CEM.

(6) Participate with target exploitation (TAREX) elements to fully integrate the exploitation of specified C-E items.

(7) Participate with medical, CBRN, and special operations units for coordinating the delivery of CB samples through MI channels to the Army Medical Laboratory (AML).

   b.   Subordinate Commands:

(1) Each Corps will—

     (a) Designate and operate collection points. Report locations of collection points where CEM will be stored and amounts and types stored at each location. Forward reports to Commander, CMEC, with an information copy to the J-2/G-2 and J-4/G4s. The collection point will receive, store and, only upon direction, dispose or issue CEM.

     (b) Designate and operate ammunition storage areas for the storage of captured ammunition and explosive items, as required. Store captured chemical munitions similarly to US chemical munitions. Report locations of ammunition storage areas and amounts and types stored to commander, CMEC, with an information copy to J-2/G-2 and J-4/G4.

     (c) Provide necessary logistics support to evacuate CEM and CB samples needed for intelligence operations, or other purposes, from collection points to the CMEC.

     (d) Ensure all CEM is promptly tagged.

     (e) Provide logistics and administrative support for all TECHINT assets operating within their areas.

(2) CBRN reconnaissance units, special operations units, and medical units are responsible for the transfer of CB samples to TEs or TECHINT collection teams at Corps, or directly to the AML.

4. PROCEDURES:

   a.   Procedures for handling and processing CEM.

(1) The recovery and evacuation of CEM is a command responsibility at all levels. The prescribed method of evacuation is through normal logistics channels and in accordance with priorities established in Tab A and Tab B to this appendix.

(2) Enemy materiel captured by US military personnel is the property of the United States and must be protected from pilferage, cannibalizing, and souvenir hunters. Commanders at all levels will provide adequate security for CEM until it has been screened by TECHINT personnel.

(3) Specific intelligence collection requirements and Top Ten End Item requirements items of enemy materiel for which the tactical commander and intelligence agencies have a need are listed at Tab A and Tab B to this appendix. These tabs will be published upon execution of the OPLAN.

     (a) When items listed in Tab A and Tab B or any of their updates are captured or otherwise obtained, commanders will ensure that the acquisition is reported through intelligence channels to the Corps TECHINT LNE to commander, CMEC, with an information copy to J-2/G-2.

(b) Report as in (a) above (at a PRIORITY precedence) the capture of standard types of foreign materiel that have been apparently modified in a major way or are having a greater impact on combat operations than expected. These items will be evacuated to COSCOM collection points by available backhaul capabilities on a PRIORITY basis. Equipment will be held pending further disposition instructions from the J-2 through the Corps TECHINT LNE.

(c) The capture of items listed in Tab A and Tab B will be reported by IMMEDIATE precedence through intelligence channels and expeditiously evacuated to at least the supporting collection point to await further disposition instructions from J-2.

(d) Report as in (a) above (at a ROUTINE precedence) all CEM. These items will be evacuated to collection points by available backhaul capabilities on a space-available basis. They will be held at the collection point until screened by TECHINT personnel. Disposition will be per paragraph 4d below.

(e) The J-2, in coordination with the J-4, is the focal point for evacuation of key items of intelligence interest to CONUS for national exploitation.

(4) The assessment of CEM below division and separate brigade levels will be limited. Their primary responsibility is the recovery, reporting the capture, and initial evacuation of enemy materiel from the capture location to the nearest collection point. Exception is for medical supplies which will be handled through medical supply channels. Significant items of CEM which cannot be evacuated, either because of the tactical situation or due to their size, will be left in place and reported immediately.

(5) Assessment of CEM at division and separate brigade level is performed by intelligence and operations personnel to the extent necessary to determine the immediate tactical significance of the materiel. Assessment at this level does not replace the need for detailed evaluation and analysis of CEM by technical specialists from the CMEC. For this reason, the prompt evacuation of significant items of CEM must not be delayed.

(6) Screening and preliminary field assessment of CEM is performed by CMEC TECHINT collection teams. These teams will operate in the Corps areas and are attached to the Corps MI Brigade. When required, these teams can also provide assistance to capturing units. Assessment functions are normally carried out at the Corps support area collection points. Items of intelligence interest or items needed to fill other requirements by the CMEC are selected for evacuation. Selected items will be evacuated to the CMEC, or a designated location, by collection point personnel through logistics channels.

(7) CEM evacuated to the CMEC is subjected to detailed examination and evaluation:

(a) Determine enemy materiel threats, performance capabilities, and limitations.

(b) Produce information from which countermeasures may be developed.

(c) Provide inputs continuously to the national and integrated S&TI program in accordance with DIA and theater policies.

(d) Provide intelligence that can be of timely use to the tactical commander.

b. Materiel Requiring Special Handling.

(1) C-E Equipment. All CEM in this category must be evacuated immediately with their dial settings, frequencies, and so forth, and recorded and sent to the supporting EW

unit by the quickest and most secure means possible. TECHINT and other specialized personnel will evacuate this materiel to Corps support area collection points for screening.

(2) Ammunition and Explosives. The complete recovery and expeditious evacuation of enemy ammunition and components is essential to the identification of known or new enemy weapons systems and the threat posed by each. EOD teams are responsible for preparing PRETECHREPs on first-time-seen enemy ammunition or explosives. If there are no TECHINT personnel to assist in the area, EOD teams will also be responsible for preparing COMTECHREPs.

(3) Medical Materiel. Medical materiel normally will not be destroyed. It will be left in place if it cannot be evacuated. Handle in accordance with normal Class VIII procedures.

(4) Significant Items: All intelligence requirements specified in Tab A and Tab B will be afforded special handling as described in paragraph 4a above.

(5) Technical Documents: Captured or recovered technical documents consist of firing tables, logbooks, packing slips, and other documentation. If the tactical situation does not permit the equipment to be evacuated, the documents will be forwarded to the CMEC and will include a description of the equipment.

(6) CB Samples. See Tab D to this appendix.

c. Requirements.

(1) DIA provides national intelligence requirements for CEM to the theater. In-theater intelligence requirements for enemy materiel are submitted through J-2 and G-2.

(2) In-theater operational and training requirements for other than Army subordinate units are submitted through J-3 to the J-2 for review, approval, and assignment of priority.

(3) The intelligence requirements are published in Tab A and Tab B.

d. Disposition.

(1) Items required in support of operational requirements or for distribution to host country forces will be separately designated by the J-3. Tab C to this Appendix describes this equipment.

(2) Items determined to have no intelligence significance (J-2) and no operational value (J-3) would then be identified and reported through logistics channels to the J-4. Items will be retained within designated collection points for further disposition by the J-4. No items will be released for war trophies until released by J-2.

e. Destruction. The destruction of CEM, excluding medical items, will be accomplished only in the event that recapture is imminent, due to its location, or in those cases where materiel is declared by EOD or TECHINT personnel to be hazardous to the safety of troops. In the event destruction of materiel is necessary, all factory markings should be carefully recorded and photographs taken, if possible, before the materiel is destroyed.
OFFICIAL:
TABS:
A = Top Ten Priority Items (TBP)
B = General Collection Requirements (TBP)
C = Equipment Releasable to Allies (TBP)
D = Chemical, Biological, and Biomedical Sampling

Appendix B

TECHNICAL INTELLIGENCE REPORTS

Note: This appendix contains the example provided in FM 34-54, *Technical Intelligence*, 30 January 1998, Appendix E, and is extracted in its entirety.

This appendix describes the nine basic reports used by battlefield TECHINT analysts.

1. SALUTE report
2. Preliminary Technical Report (PRETECHREP)
3. Multi-Service Complementary Technical Intelligence Report (COMTECHREP)
4. Detailed Technical Report (DETECHREP)
5. Technical Intelligence Update Report
6. Technical Intelligence Summary (TECHSUM)
7. Technical Intelligence Report (TIR)
8. Special Technical Reports. These reports are generated in response to requests for information. The formats vary by request and usually address a specific question or requirement from a TECHINT consumer.
9. Other Equipment Information Reports. These reports focus on aspects of equipment that do not necessarily relate to intelligence needs per se. For example, the theater commander may have a war trophy policy that permits units to evacuate certain equipment to their home stations for static displays. These reports may include driver's instructions, handling considerations, render-safe procedures, and demilitarization standards for equipment.

SALUTE (Size, Activity, Location, Unit/Uniform, Time, Equipment) REPORT

The SALUTE report is an oral or written report prepared by the acquiring units or intermediate command echelons. It is used to report rapidly, by electrical or other means, the capture of foreign materiel. These reports are forwarded to either the TECHINT LNEs at Corps, other TECHINT LNEs, or directly to the CMEC. As a result of this information, a TECHINT team could be dispatched or the CEM could be moved to the Corps CMEC or the theater CMEC. An example of a completed SALUTE report is shown below.

SALUTE REPORT

TO: G-2 V Corps DTG: 230900Z Aug 98
FROM: G-2 24th Inf Div (Mech) REPORT NO: 07-0623

1. SIZE: NA.
2. ACTIVITY: Capture of shoulder-fired laser target designator by 1/64th Armor Bn 2d Bde 24th Inf Div (Mech) (include capturing unit).
3. LOCATION: Town of Al-Dahran (UTM EH556937) (as a minimum always give grid coordinates).
4. UNIT: 3d Republican Guards Regiment (include enemy unit if known).
5. TIME: Item captured on 230230Z AUG 98 (always use ZULU time).
6. EQUIPMENT: One laser target designator and sighting device (give best possible description).

PRELIMINARY TECHNICAL REPORT (PRETECHREP)

The PRETECHREP contains a general description of the CEE. It alerts the CMEC, other technical elements, and the tactical units to significant technical information of immediate tactical importance. It can also be used for reporting inventories at collection points through intelligence channels so that location, quantities, and type of equipment can be monitored. Below is an example of a PRETECHREP. Corps TECHINT teams and possibly CMEC teams will prepare a PRETECHREP on all CEM after preliminary screening. This report is first transmitted by radio directly to the Corps TECHINT LNE, from the captured equipment site. It is then forwarded to the CMEC. The report will normally be treated as unclassified during this transmission. The CMEC's technical analysts determine what is of importance from the report and give the team instructions through the LNE on what items need more detailed reporting or evacuation. During this time the team will collect all documents off the CEE and will record the following on the PRETECHREP:

PRETECHREP

A. Type of equipment and quantity.
B. Date and time of capture.
C. Location (map reference).
D. Capturing unit and circumstances of capture.
E. Enemy formation from which captured and origin.
F. Brief description with serial numbers and, if possible, manufacturer.
G. Technical characteristics with an immediate value, including information or any photographs available.
H. Time and origin of message.
I. Present location of CEE.

Things to consider when filling out a PRETECHREP:

- All radio frequencies of communication equipment.

- All serial markings of important equipment.

- The battle damage done to the CEE.

- These information requirements and actions will be taken at all CEE sites.

- The radio frequencies will be sent only by secured means.

COMPLEMENTARY TECHNICAL INTELLIGENCE REPORT (COMTECHREP)

The COMTECHREP is categorized by types, depending on what type of CEE is being reported. The COMTECHREP contains a more detailed description of the CEE than the PRETECHREP. It alerts the CMEC, other technical elements, and the tactical units to significant detailed technical information of immediate tactical and technical importance.

Corps TECHINT teams, and possibly CMEC teams, will prepare a COMTECHREP on all CEM that the CMEC tells it to do. If the TECHINT collection team is out of contact with the CMEC, it will follow the TECHINT collection plan and use its best judgment on reporting.

This report is first transmitted normally by secure computer data transmission over landline to the Corps TECHINT LNE from the team's base. If possible, it is transmitted from the CEE site over secure computer or radio data transmission via satellite. It is then transmitted to the CMEC. The report normally will be treated as classified during this transmission. All electronic images of the CEE and computer scanning of critical CED will be transmitted with the COMTECHREP. If data transmission is not on hand, the report will be transmitted by the nearest message center at no less than PRIORITY precedence.

MULTI-SERVICE COMPLEMENTARY TECHNICAL INTELLIGENCE REPORT

The MULTI-SERVICE COMTECHREP is used to report all items that are not associated with explosive ordnance. This report is submitted as soon as possible. Below is an example of a Multi-Service COMTECHREP.

MULTI-SERVICE COMTECHREP

A. Date found and location (map reference).
B. Type of equipment and quantity.
C. Origin.
D. Description with distinguishing marks (additional details).
E. Condition of equipment.
F. Technical characteristics of immediate tactical value (additional details).
G. Recommended disposal.
H. Name plates photographed.
I. Photographs taken.
J. Other information.
K. Designation of TECHINT collection team doing this initial exploitation.
L. Time and origin of message.

COMTECHREP - TYPE B

The COMTECHREP - Type B is used to report information about explosive ordnance. TECHINT teams prepare these reports, normally done by the EOD member of the team. EOD companies will also prepare them in absence of TECHINT personnel or when required by higher headquarters. This report must be as complete and detailed as possible. EOD personnel prepare and send this report by the fastest means through an EOD control unit. The CMEC coordinates with EOD battalions to receive copies of these reports as soon as possible.

Note: Initial overall classification of EOD Reports. Non-nuclear (COMTECHREP B) will be in accordance with OPNAVINST S5513.3B-24.1.

The initial classification of the COMTECHREP B with RSP is Confidential and will not be released to non-US personnel without the written consent of Commanding Officer, NAVEODTECHDIV.

A complete and accurate report is essential; lives of other EOD personnel rely on this report, strive for the most complete report possible. However, when a detailed report might result in serious delay and the items are of extreme significance, complete as much of the report as possible. Items of EOD interest will at a minimum be photographed (with electronic imaging systems if available), X-rays (digital) and have detailed drawings with measurements (metric). Figure E-4 shows an example of a COMTECHREP - TYPE B.

The unit completing the report will distribute copies of the COMTECHREP - TYPE B (EOD Report) to all deployed US EOD units and provide copies to:

Commander
USATECHDET
2008 Stump Neck Road
Indian Head, MD 20640

Commander
USAARDEC
ATTN: AMSTA-AR-FSX
Picatinny Arsenal, NJ 07806-5000

Commanding Officer
NAVEODTECHDIV
2008 Stump Neck Road
Indian Head, MD 20640

Commander
NGIC
ATTN: IANGIC-RMS
220 7th Street, NE
Charlottesville, VA 22901-5396

COMTECHREP-TYPE B (EOD Report)

PRIORITY

FM: XXXX ORD CO (EOD)
TO: XXXX (JEODOC)
INFO: CDRUSATECHDET INDIAN HEAD MD
NAVEODTECHDIV INDIAN HEAD MD//
FSTC CHARLOTTESVILLE VA//AIFRCB/AIFIM//
DIA WASHINGTON DC//DT2C/DT-3B//

BT
SECRET/NOFORN/WNINTEL
WARNING NOTICE - SENSITIVE INTELLIGENCE SOURCES OR METHODS
INVOLVED
SUBJ: COMTECHREP
REF A. MSG XXX SUBJECT: PRETECHREP

a.   ( ) Date and location of acquisition, acquired by, and for whom.
b.   ( ) Nationality, designation, and identification marks.
c.   ( ) Description.
d.   ( ) Overall length, including fuze, tail, vanes, or control surfaces and fittings; measurement of various states (if there are several).
e.   ( ) Maximum diameter of each state (if there are several).
f.   ( ) Shape, design, and internal configuration (streamlining shells).
g.   ( ) Span of vanes and control surfaces.
h.   ( ) Number, relative positions, and dimensions (width, length, size, and/or configuration of control surfaces).
i.   ( ) Thickness of casing at —
    (1)   ( ) nose.
    (2)   ( ) slides.
    (3)   ( ) base.
j.   ( ) Type and materials of body and control surfaces.

k. ( ) Color and markings of —
    (1)   ( ) nose.
    (2)   ( ) body.
    (3)   ( ) tail and vanes.
l. ( ) Weight —
    (1)   ( ) total, including propellant.
    (2)   ( ) of filling.
m. ( ) Nature of filling. If chemical or biological warfare in nature, give method of filling, for example, bomblets or massive fill; specify method of delivery, such as spray, roundburst, or airburst. For antitank missiles with high explosive antitank (HEAT) warheads, give full details of cone-liner materials, cone angle, and diameter. For antitank missiles with non-HEAT warheads, give full description of the warhead.
n. ( ) Type of missile guidance system and method of stabilization environment (control and guidance radars, acquisition radar); frequencies used for reception response (in case of a transponder); and proximity fuze (if there is one). Electronic countermeasures and electronic counter-countermeasures equipment and/or chaff-dispensing equipment.
o. ( ) Sensors.
p. ( ) Diameter of radome and size of homing dish, if fitted.
q. ( ) Dimensions (internal and external) of wave guides in the homing head and wave guides and/or aerials in the wings or body, and the technology used.
r. ( ) Homing head, transducer design, and shape and size (torpedoes).
s. ( ) Method of propulsion and propeller data (torpedoes).
t. ( ) Detonating system, fuzing system (nose, tail, or transverse) and firing mechanism details.
u. ( ) Type of suspension, giving details of devices used, such as electrically operated hoods or release gear.
v. ( ) Antihandling or booby-trap devices.
w. ( ) Other information (to include estimate of time required to prepare item for shipment to TECHINT center or designated industrial firm for detailed analysis).
x. ( ) Name of officer in command of technical team making examination.
y. ( ) Time and origin of message.
z. ( ) Energy used for mobile systems other than propulsions.
aa. ( ) Estimate of time required for completion.

Note: If feasible, a preliminary set of photographs should be sent with the report.

(Classification)

Note: The subject and each paragraph and subparagraph must be classified individually, but not higher than the classification of the entire message.

NINE LINE UXO/IED SPOT REPORT

When mines, explosives, or other UXOs are found, report them to the unit's tactical operations center (TOC) using the following format: An example of a Nine Line UXO/IED Spot Report is shown below:

Nine Line UXO/IED SPOT Report

Line 1. Date-Time Group (DTG) the item was discovered.

Line 2. Reporting Activity (unit identification code) and location (grid of UXO).

Line 3. Contact Method: Radio frequency, call sign, point of contact, and telephone number.

Line 4. Type of Ordnance: Dropped, projected, placed, or thrown. If known, give the size of the hazard area and number of items. Without touching, disturbing, or approaching (tripwire) the item, include details about size, shape, color, and condition (intact or leaking).

Line 5. CBRN Contamination: If present, be as specific as possible.

Line 6. Resources Threatened: Report any threatened equipment, facilities, or other assets.

Line 7. Impact on Mission: Provide a short description of your current tactical situation and how the presence of the UXO affects your status.

Line 8. Protective Measures: Describe any measures taken to protect personnel and equipment.

Line 9. Recommended Priority (see table below): Recommend a priority for response by EOD technicians or engineers.

Priority	Basis
Immediate	Stops the unit's maneuver and mission capability or threatens critical assets vital to the mission.
Indirect	Slows the unit's maneuver and mission capability or threatens critical assets important to the mission.
Minor	Reduces the unit's maneuver and mission capability or threatens non-critical assets of value.
No Threat	Has little or no affect on the unit's capabilities or assets.

Table B-1. Priority Listings

DETAILED TECHNICAL REPORT (DETECHREP)

The DETECHREP normally is prepared at the CMEC by the Exploitation Company, with the assistance of the national S&TI analysis personnel at the CMEC. The DECTECHREP normally is classified. The CM&D section of the Exploitation Company sends the DETECHREP to the national S&TI community. They also send a summary of the report to theater units.

TECHNICAL INTELLIGENCE UPDATE REPORT

The TECHINT Update Report is a one- to two-paragraph report on an item of equipment that has an impact on tactical operations. The report comes from information provided in PRETECHREPs and COMTECHREPs, and is unclassified. The goal of the report is to reach the lowest level—the Soldier—with information of value to the Soldier. The CM&D section of the Operations Company sends the report by electronic message and computer data transmission.

TECHNICAL INTELLIGENCE SUMMARY

The TECHINT Summary is a collection of information on more than one item of equipment that has an impact on theater tactical operations. The information comes from PRETECHREPs and COMTECHREPs from over a period of time or from a large CEE location. The report normally is unclassified, but if put into an overall intelligence summary, it can be classified. The CM&D section of the Exploitation Company sends the report by electronic message and computer data transmission to the CMEC. The CMEC then makes dissemination to the lowest possible level with JTF C I assets.

TECHNICAL INTELLIGENCE REPORT (TIR)

The TIR is a critical report which goes to the highest levels of the intelligence hierarchy. The report comes from information from PRETECHREPs, COMTECHREPs, and DETECHREPs. This report is always classified and follows the format in DIAM 58-13. The CM&D section sends TIRs by electronic message to the CMEC. The CMEC disseminates them to the highest and lowest intelligence units and agencies possible.

This page intentionally left blank.

Appendix C

CHECKLISTS

1. Pre-Combat Checks
2. Pre-Combat Inspections
3. Photography
4. TECHINT Operations and Procedures
5. TECHINT Operations Checklist for Maneuver S-2

1. Pre-Combat Checks (PCCs)

PCCs are procedures for all individuals assigned to a convoy to determine if equipment required for a mission is available and serviceable. PCCs are effective only if they are organized and conducted using an up-to-date checklist. This section provides suggested checklists for leaders, specialty teams and individuals. Use these checklists as a guideline. The type of unit, equipment, operational area and mission will dictate additions, substitutions and deletions. Follow through is essential, missing or unserviceable equipment must be rapidly reported, repaired or exchanged. These checks should be scheduled soon after the warning order is issued at a time where individuals are released from other duties.

2. Pre-Combat Inspections (PCIs)

PCIs are the series of inspections scheduled early in the preparation sequence to insure that all PCCs have been performed properly and that all vehicles, weapons, communications, special and individual equipment are available and functional. These PCIs are most effective when organized and conducted to exacting standards by first line supervisors with systematic spot checks made by the senior convoy leadership.

FM 4-01.45, MCRP 4-11.3H, NTTP 4-01.3, AFTTP(I) 3-2.58, *Multi-Service Tactics, Techniques, and Procedures for Tactical Convoy Operations*, has many checklists that may be of value to a TECHINT team operating in a field environment.

3. Photography

Intelligence may be assisted by photographic methods. High quality pictures can provide permanent records so that detailed interpretation of the collected data can be made. Cameras record full details of the target instantly, and photographs should be made of all targets worthy of observation. Two different types of TECHINT photography are usually conducted.

- Base-line photography.

- Detailed photography.

a. Base-line photography: If possible, photographers should take shots from the eight basic directions. Figure C-1 displays an example of using the eight basic directions against a maritime target.

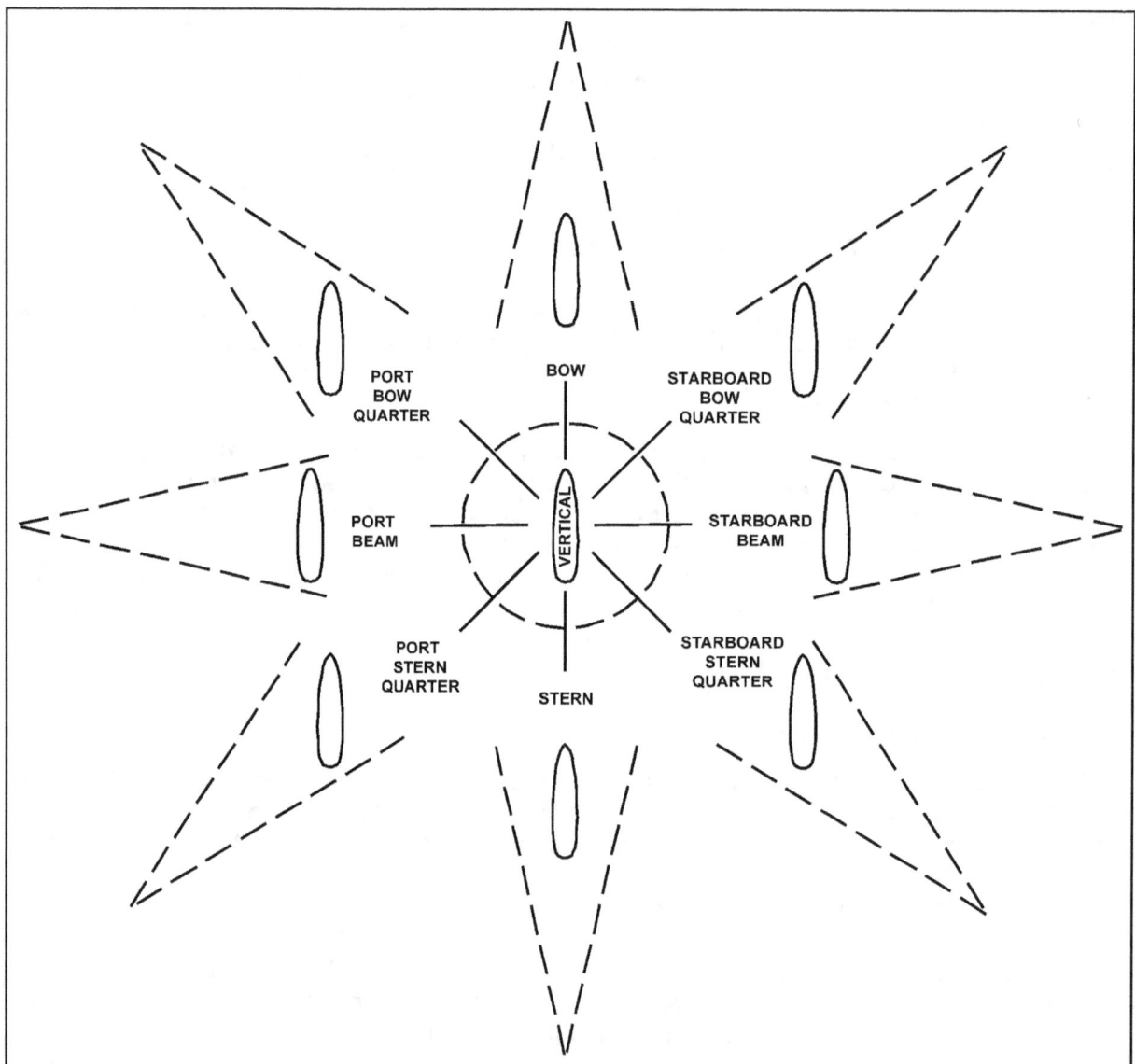

Figure C-1. Eight Basic Directions

b. Detailed Photography: Detailed photography involves photographic methods that are more detailed and time consuming. Detailed photography collects information on characteristics such as data plates, nomenclatures, and any other specific information of intelligence value.

c. Photolog Diagram: The photolog diagram provides a description and location of a target and information necessary for analysts to understand the photographer's location and circumstances relative to the target. Generally, a photolog includes the following items (see Table C-1 for an example):

    (1) Line item.
    (2) Date/time group (with the appropriate time zone designator).
    (3) Description of the subject (object) being photographed.

(4) Location of the subject (preferably a GPS fix in lat long).

(5) Distance to the subject (from the photographer).

(6) Bearing to the subject (from the photographer). Make sure to denote magnetic or true.

(7) Photograph naming/numbering convention(s).

(8) Environmental conditions.

(9) Traffic/egress/approach.

	Date / Time	Description	Location	Distance	Bearing
1	061551ZDEC05	Mobile Scud Firing Panel	BIAP (N33 15' 37" E044 14' 3.9")	6 FT	360 deg M
2	061552ZDEC05	Mobile Scud Hydraulic Elevating System	BIAP (N33 15' 37" E044 14' 3.9")	30 FT	270 deg M

Table C-1. Photolog Example

4. TECHINT Operations and Procedures

The following list provides TECHINT analysts at the team level with a basic guideline for conducting initial on-site exploitation of CEM:

- Mission preparation.
- Link-up with supported unit.
- Leader's reconnaissance.
- EOD establishes safe entry and exit points and minimize hazards on target. No one will enter the site until briefed by EOD on possible hazards.
- Depending on the situation, CBRN analysts conduct chemical, biological, radiological, nuclear, or high-yield explosive (CBRNE) hazard analysis.
- Other personnel will follow as required by the mission to conduct exploitation.
- Base line photographs.
- Measurements.
- Specific exploitation.
- Report findings to next higher command.
- Prepare and evacuate CEM as directed.
- Conduct battle damage assessment (BDA) as directed.

5. TECHINT Operations Checklist for Maneuver S-2

TECHINT OPERATIONS CYCLE		S-2 SPECIFIC TASKS
TECHINT TEMPLATING	Through all-source analysis, CMEC template where items of TECHINT interest are most likely to be found on the battlefield.	Provide updated order of battle information for specific area of operations (AO) to next higher echelon.
UNIT NOTIFICATION	Through operations channels appropriate units are notified that items may be within their AO.	Maintain updated captured materiel (CM) TECHINT requirements.
CAPTURE	Service member either captures or observes an item of possible TECHINT interest and does not tamper with it.	Prior to all missions, ensure Soldiers are educated on current TECHINT requirements. Provide enemy equipment reference manuals/photos. Maintain CEM tags and provide them to Soldiers prior to missions.
SALUTE REPORT	SALUTE report is generated on the CEM and forwarded to next higher.	Check SALUTE report for accuracy and ensure it is forwarded.
SECURITY COORDINATION	CEM **MUST NOT** be touched or tampered with in any way until the equipment is photographed or positions recorded.	Coordinate with S-3 for security or continued observation of the CEM and ensure the item is not tampered with in any way.
CAPTURE REPORT	Capture report is generated on the CEM and forwarded to next higher and EOD channels.	Generate capture report and forward it to the next higher echelon.
SEGREGATE	Items of potential interest will be identified based on the TECHINT collection requirements and segregated from other CEM.	Segregate items of potential interest based on the TECHINT collection requirements from other CEM.
DESTRUCTION	The capturing unit may be ordered to destroy CEM.	Coordinate with S-3/S-4 for organic evacuation of CEM.
TRANSPORTATION	The capturing unit may be ordered to evacuate CEM with organic equipment to next higher echelon or temporary holding area via backhaul.	Coordinate with S-3/S-4 for organic evacuation of CEM. Establish temporary holding area.
STORAGE	The capturing unit may be ordered to safeguard the CEM with organic assets until TECHINT teams arrive.	Coordinate with S-3 for security or continued observation of the CEM for organic evacuation.

Table C-2. TECHINT Operations Checklist for Maneuver S-2

FM 2-22.401/NTTP 2-01.4/AFTTP(I) 3-2.63   9 June 2006

Appendix D

FOREIGN LANGUAGE TEXT RECOGNITION

Note: This appendix contains a portion of the example provided in FM 34-54, *Technical Intelligence*, 30 January 1998, Appendix G.

When TECHINT personnel are able to correctly identify foreign languages used in documents or equipment, it has two immediate benefits. First, it helps identify the equipment or type of document and where or who is using it. Second, it ensures that TECHINT personnel request the correct linguistic support.

This appendix contains language identification hints that will enable TECHINT personnel to quickly identify some of the many languages used in documents, on equipment plates, and on other materiel. TECHINT personnel can speed up the entire battlefield TECHINT process by following the guidance herein.

The language identification hints were compiled by NGIC. There are thousands of languages and dialects in use in the world today; therefore, this material is not complete. The following include examples of the use of language identification during TECHINT operations.

A TECHINT team discovers an ADA system that looks like a Russian ZPU-4 ADA gun. But on closer examination, the technical analysis identifies Chinese characters on a data plate and on the tires. This could mean that this ADA gun is from China, and this observation needs to be reported to TECHINT elements and to the CMEC.

TECHINT personnel find a document in Arabic, but the country they are in speak and write only Spanish. This document could be of intelligence value and would require being reported to TECHINT elements and to document exploitation (DOCEX) personnel.

LANGUAGE SYSTEMS

The world's written languages can be divided into alphabet languages and character languages. The only present-day character system is the Chinese system, which has been borrowed by other languages. But there are many alphabets. The most important alphabets currently in use are—

- The Roman alphabet (used by English and many other languages).
- The Cyrillic alphabet (used by Russian, some other Slavic languages, and most of the minority languages of Russia).
- The Arabic alphabet (used in the Middle East and other areas influenced by Islam).
- Other alphabets exist, but their use is more restricted. (Figure D-1 shows some of these spoken languages and some of the locations where they are spoken.)
- The Hebrew alphabet for Hebrew and Yiddish; the Greek alphabet for Greek.
- The Devanagari alphabet for Sanskrit and other languages of India.
- In addition, there are special alphabets for languages like Georgian, Telugu, the other Dravidian languages in southern India, Laos, and other languages in southeast Asia, and Amharic in Ethiopia.

Illustrations of the main alphabets are normally available in standard desktop dictionaries. Many unusual scripts are illustrated in Romanization Guides, revised and enlarged edition, put out by the Office of the Geographer, Directorate for Functional Research, Bureau of Intelligence and Research, US Department of State, and the US Board on Geographic Names, dated 1 April 1972.

Reliable detailed information about foreign languages for people who cannot actually read them is available in manuals compiled for professional librarians. These manuals can be found at your local library.

Language	Location
Chinese	People's Republic of China, Taiwan, Hong Kong, Thailand
English	United States, Canada, Great Britain, Ireland, Australia, New Zealand
Spanish	Spain, South America, Central America, Mexico
Hindi	North Central India
Russian	Soviet Union, Europe
Arabic	Saudi Arabia, Yemen, South Yemen, United Arab Emirates, Oman, Kuwait, Bahrain, Qatar, Iraq, Syria, Jordan, Lebanon, Egypt, Sudan, Libya, Tunisia, Algeria, Morocco
Portuguese	Portugal, Brazil, Africa, Asia
Japanese	Japan
German	Germany, Austria, Switzerland
Urdu	Pakistan, India
French	France, Belgium, Switzerland, Canada, Morocco, Tunisia, Algeria, Lebanon, Syria, Laos, Cambodia, Vietnam
Korean	Korea, China, Japan
Italian	Italy, Switzerland
Vietnamese	Vietnam
Turkish	Turkey, Bulgaria, Greece, Cyprus
Persian (Farsi, Dari)	Iran, Afghanistan (Tadzhik, USSR)
Polish	Poland, United States, Soviet Union
Ukrainian	Ukrainian SSR
Rumanian	Romania, Moldavian SSR
Serbian (Croatian)	Yugoslavia
Pashto	Afghanistan, Northwest Pakistan
Czech (Slovak)	Czechoslovakia
Dutch	Netherlands, Suriname, Belgium
Hungarian	Hungary, Romania, Czechoslovakia, Yugoslavia
	Danish (Norwegian) Denmark, Norway
Bulgarian	Bulgaria
Swedish	Sweden
Belorussian	Belorussian SSR
Finnish	Finland
Albanian	Albania, Yugoslavia
Lithuanian	Lithuanian SSR
Latvian	Latvian SSR
Slovenian	Slovenia (Northwest Yugoslavia)
Estonian	Estonian SSR
Macedonian	Macedonia (Yugoslavia)

Figure D-1. Partial List of Spoken Languages and Locations Where They Are Spoken

ROMAN ALPHABET LANGUAGES

The most complex language recognition problem is to distinguish between the numerous languages that use the Roman alphabet. The 26-letter alphabet is used here as the basic alphabet. The other Roman alphabet languages use these same letters, but many use fewer than 26 and a few use more.

Unfortunately, just because a letter is not used is not a very useful language recognition criterion. This is because it is difficult to know whether a letter is absent because it is never used or because it simply was not needed to write the text in question.

Five of the letters <a, e, i, o, u> are referred to collectively as "vowels," while the rest are called collectively "consonants." The rules designating letters as vowels or consonants vary from language to language. Some languages, for instance, consider <l>, <r>, or <y> to be vowels. Most of the Roman alphabet languages modify letters by putting extra marks above, in, or below them. **These marks are called diacritics. They are among the best criteria for language recognition.**

DIACRITICS

A diacritical mark or diacritic, sometimes called an accent mark, is a mark added to a letter to alter a word's pronunciation or to distinguish between similar words. A diacritical mark can appear above or below the letter to which it is added, or in some other position; however, note that not all such marks are diacritical. For example, in English, the tittle (dot) on the letters i and j is not a diacritical mark, but rather part of the letter itself. Further, a mark may be diacritical in one language, but not in another; for example, in Catalan, Portuguese or Spanish, u and ü are considered the same letter, while in German, Estonian, Hungarian, Turkish or Azeri they are considered to be separate letters.

The main usage of a diacritic is to change the phonetic meaning of the letter, but the term is also used in a more general sense of changing the meaning of the letter or even the whole word.

1. Types of Diacritic

The following are types of diacritic:

(˙) *anunaasika* superdot

(.) *anusvaara* subdot, used in Sanskrit

(¸) *cedilla*

(̨) *ogonek* or "Polish hook"

(°) *kr'oužek* or ring; unlike in Czech, in the Scandinavian languages this is not considered a diacritic but an integral part of the character å.

(˘) breve; part of the character when used in Esperanto

(ˇ) caron or *háček* ("little hook" in Czech). In Slovak it is called *mäkčeň* ("softener" or "palatalization mark"), in Slovenian *strešica* ("little roof"), in Croatian *kvačica* ("little hook").

(^) circumflex, part of the character when used in Esperanto, also in Slovak is used on "o" and it is called *vokáň*

(‾) macron

(¨) diaeresis (also dieresis) or umlaut, a diacritic in some languages (such as German), but part of the character in the Swedish and Russian languages.

(`) grave accent

(´) acute accent

(˝) double acute accent

(ʽ) *spiritus asper* or rough breathing mark

(ʼ) *spiritus lenis* or smooth (or soft) breathing mark

Marks that are sometimes diacritics, but also have other uses, are:

(|) bar through the basic letter

(,) comma

(~) tilde

(˜) titlo, used to indicate abbreviation in the early Cyrillic alphabet

(') apostrophe

(:) colon, used to attach native affixes (such as case markers) to foreign words and abbreviations

(-) hyphen - in English, hyphens can be used to break words between syllables, to resolve ambiguities in pronunciation

2. Usage

a.   Catalan has grave, acute, cedilla and diaeresis.

b.   Several Chinese romanizations use umlaut, but only on u (ü). In Hanyu Pinyin, the four tones of Mandarin Chinese are denoted by the macron, acute, caron and grave diacritics.

c.   Czech has acute, caron and ring.

d.   Dutch uses diaeresis. For example in ruïne it means that the u and i are separately pronounced in their usual way, and not in the way that the combination ui is normally pronounced. Thus it works as a separation sign and not as an indication for an alternative version of the i. Diacritics can be used for emphasis (érg koud for very cold) or for disambiguation between the numeral one (één appel, one apple) and the indefinite article (een appel, an apple). Grave and acute accents are used on a very small number of words, mostly loanwords.

e.   In Estonian, carons in š or ž may appear only in foreign proper names and loanwords, but may be also substituted with sh or zh in some texts. Apostrophe can be used in declension of some foreign names to separate the stem from any declension endings; e.g., Monet' or Monet'sse for the genitive case and illative case, respectively, for (the famous painter) "Monet".

f.   French uses grave, acute, circumflex, cedilla and diaeresis. However, not all diacritics occur on all vowels in French:

g.   Acute (accent aigu) only occurs on e (é, pronounced /e/)

h.   Grave (accent grave) occurs on e (è, pronounced /ɛ/), a (à), and u (ù)

i.   Circumflex (accent circonflexe) occurs on all vowels: e (ê, pronounced /ɛ/), a (â, pronounced /ɑ/), i (î), o (ô, pronounced /o/), and u (û; if occurring in the combination eû, pronounced /ø/)

j.   Cedilla (cédille) is used only under the c (ç, pronounced /s/). It is used in cases in which a c is soft before a, o, or u, such as ça (pronounced /sa/, not /ka/).

k.   Diaeresis (tréma) occurs on e (ë), i (ï), u (ü), and y (ÿ). The diaeresis only occurs on y in a few proper nouns, including Louÿs and L'Haÿ-les-Roses. The mark's function is to indicate that the vowel is pronounced separately from the one just before it.

l.   Diacritics are sometimes omitted from capitalized letters, especially in France.

m.   Not all French diacritics affect pronunciation. However, all cases in which they do have been noted in the foregoing.

n.   Finnish uses a colon to decline loanwords and abbreviations; e.g., USA:han for the illative case of "USA". Also characters ä and ö are part of the Finnish alphabet (a and o with Umlaut).

o.   German has the Umlaut (¨). This can be used over a, o, or u to indicate vowel modification. For instance: Ofen (/'o:fən/); Öfen (/'ø:fən/), which in this case makes the difference between singular and plural ("oven"/"ovens"). The sign originated in a superscript e; a handwritten Sütterlin e resembles two parallel vertical lines, like an umlaut.

p.   Irish uses acute accent to indicate that the vowel is long. It is known as síneadh fada in Irish.

q.   Italian uses acute and grave to indicate irregular stress patterns (as in più, which would otherwise be stressed on the i) and to distinguish words that would otherwise be homographs (such as te ["you"] and tè ["tea"]). In many words, acute and grave are interchangeable.

r.   Romanized Japanese (Romaji) uses diacritics to mark long vowels. The Hepburn romanization system uses a macron to mark long vowels, and the Kunrei-shiki and Nihon-shiki systems use a circumflex.

s.   Lithuanian uses the acute, grave and tilde in dictionaries to indicate stress types in the language's pitch stress system. In general usage, where letters appear with the caron (č, š and ž) they are considered as separate letters from c, s or z and collated separately; letters with the ogonek (ą, ę, į and ų), the macron (ū) and the superdot (ė) are considered as separate letters as well, but not given a unique collation order.

t.   Portuguese uses acute (to mark stressed vowels), grave (to mark the assimilation of two identical vowels into one, now used only on A), circumflex (marks both the stress and the roundness, being deprecated in this second use), cedilla (to mark the pronunciation of C as /s/ instead of /k/ before A, O and U and tilde (to mark the nasalisation of A and O). In Brazil diaeresis is also used to differ the pronunciation of groups like qüe and güi (respectively /kwe/ and /gwi/) from que and gui (/ke/ and /gi/).

u.   Many Slavic and Baltic languages use caron to signify either palatalisation or iotation.

v.   Many Slavic languages that use the Latin alphabet have ogonek and bar.

w.   Slovak has acute, caron, circumflex (only above o) and diaresis (only above a).

x.   Spanish uses acute, diaeresis and tilde. Acute is used on a vowel in a stressed syllable in words with irregular stress patterns. It can also be used to "break" a diphthong as in tío (pronounced /'tio/, and not /tjo/ as it would be without the accent). Moreover, the acute can be used to distinguish words that otherwise are spelt alike, such as mas (= "but"} and más (= "more"), and also to distinguish interrogative and relative words otherwise spelt alike, such as donde/¿dónde? (= "where") or como/¿cómo? (= "as"/"how?"). Tilde is used on n, forming a separate letter (ñ) in the Spanish alphabet. Diaeresis is used only over u (ü) so that it is pronounced /w/ in the combinations gue and gui (where u is normally silent), for example ambigüedad. In poetry, diaeresis may be used on i and u as a way to force hiatus.

y.   Tagalog uses a hyphen after a consonant to indicate a syllable break (nag-alis /nag·a·lís/ as opposed to nagalis /na·ga·lís/). A hyphen is not necessary between two vowels, vowels being distinctly pronounced in Tagalog (tauhan /ta·ú·han/, buo /bu·ô/).

z.   Tamil does not have any diacritics in itself, but uses the Western numerals 2, 3 and 4 as diacritics to represent aspirated, voiced, and voiced-aspirated consonants when the Tamil script is used to write to long passages in Sanskrit.

aa.   Turkish uses a G-breve (Ğ), a diaeresis on two vowels (Ö and Ü) to represent rounding, a cedilla on two consonants (Ç and Ş, to represent the affricates /tS/ and /S/) and also possesses a dotted capital İ (and a dotless lowercase ı). Turkish considers each of these a separate letter, rather than a modification of existing characters, however; see Turkish alphabet for more details.

bb.   Vietnamese uses acute (dấu sắc), grave (dấu huyền), tilde (dấu ngã), dot below (dấu nặng) and hook (dấu hỏi) on vowels as tone indicators.

cc.   Welsh uses the circumflex, diaeresis, acute and grave accents on its seven vowels a, e, i, o, u, w, y. The most common is the circumflex (which it calls to bach, meaning "little roof") to denote a long vowel, usually to disambiguate it from a similar word with a short vowel. The rarer grave accent has the opposite effect, shortening vowel sounds which would usually be pronounced long. The acute accent and diaeresis are also occasionally used, to denote stress and vowel separation respectively. The w-circumflex and y-circumflex are among the most common accented characters in Welsh, but unusual in languages generally, and were until recently very hard to obtain in word-processed and HTML documents.

dd.   Modern English does not usually have diacritics, which appear only in foreign and loanwords. The letter è is an exception, used to modify the pronunciation of words ending in -ed within poetry and songs.

CYRILLIC ALPHABET LANGUAGES

The Cyrillic alphabet is used to write Russian, Ukrainian, Belorussian, and many minority languages from the former Soviet Union. It is also used to write Bulgarian and Serbian. The Cyrillic alphabet and the Roman alphabet are both derived from forms of the Greek alphabet so there is a general resemblance. Some Cyrillic letters seem to Americans to be backwards or oddly shaped. Figure D-2 shows the characters and diacritics not found in Russian. With the exception of one letter, which is only used sometimes in Russian, none of these letters appear in the normal Russian text.

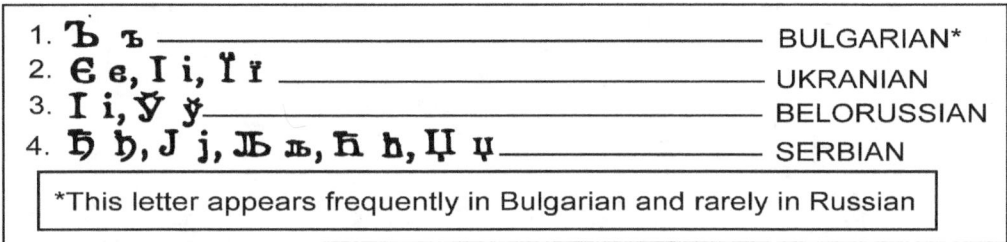

Figure D-2. Distinguishing Major Slavic Languages From Russian

SLAVIC LANGUAGES

TRANSLITERATION:

Figure D-3 shows the different forms of the Cyrillic alphabet for five principal Cyrillic alphabet languages and the recommended transliterations for each letter. Pay particular attention to the transliteration of Russian. These equivalents must be used when reporting on materiel bearing Russian nameplates. DO NOT REPORT ON FOREIGN EQUIPMENT AND DOCUMENTS USING THE ORIGINAL CYRILLIC CHARACTER. The figure classifies each letter as "C" for consonant or "N" for nonconsonant.

NOTE: In the following discussion, the letters are referred to by their numbers on the chart in Figure D-3. For example, a letter used often in Russian and never in Bulgarian is the letter 39; however, the way to be sure that it is not Bulgarian is to see if the letter 38 comes before a consonant or "C" letter. Note that letter 38 is frequent in Bulgarian and rare in Russian; moreover, when letter 38 occurs in Russian, it always occurs before an "N" letter.

RUSSIAN: Russian is the most frequently encountered Cyrillic alphabet language and should always be the prime suspect. The key to recognizing Russian is the fact that it uses both letter 12 and letter 39 and does not use letter 13 at all.

BULGARIAN: Bulgarian is perhaps the second most frequently encountered Cyrillic alphabet language and the most difficult for the nonspecialists to differentiate from Russian. Bulgarian uses fewer letters than Russian.

Proper transliteration is very important. When an analyst reads a Russian nameplate and writes down P-105A, but it is actually an R-105D (P is not P, rather "R," and < > is wrongly symbolized by A); then it results in incorrect reporting.

The column in Figure D-3 marked "Other" is not supplied with any transliteration equivalents. This column contains similar letters that are encountered in the written languages of various minority nationalities in the former USSR. These languages belong mainly to the Uralic family or the Altaic family, and a Russian linguist will be unable to make any sense out of them. Recognition of any documents in these languages as non-Slavic is a helpful first step in DOCEX.

No.	Russian		Ukrainian		Belorussian		Bulgarian		Serbian		Other
1. N	Аа	a	Аа	a	Аа	a	Аа	a	Аа	a	Ӓä Ӑă Ӕæ
2. C	Бб	b	Бб	b	Бб	b	Бб	b	Бб	b	-
3. C	Вв	v	Вв	v	Вв	v	Вв	v	Вв	v	-
4. C	Гг	g	Гг	g	Гг	g	Гг	g	Гг	g	Гг Ѓѓ
5. C	Дд	d	Дд	d	Дд	d	Дд	d	Дд	d	-
6. C	-	-	-	-	-	-	Ђђ	đ	-	-	-
7. N	Ее	e/ye	Ее	e	Ее	e/ye	Ее	e	Ее	e	Ӗӗ ӛ
8. N	Ёё	ё/yё	-	-	Ёё	ё/yё	-	-	-	-	-
9. N	-	-	Єє	ye	-	-	-	-	-	-	-
10. C	Жж	zh	Жж	zh	Жж	zh	Жж	zh	Жж	ž	Җҗ Жж
11. C	Зз	z	Зз	z	Зз	z	Зз	z	Зз	z	Зз Ӡӡ
12. N	Ии	i	Ии	y	-	-	Ии	i	Ии	i	Йй Ӣӣ
13. N	-	-	Іі	i	Іі	i	-	-	-	-	Іі Її
14. N	-	-	Її	yi	-	-	-	-	-	-	-
15. C	Йй	y	Йй	y	Йй	y	Йй	y	-	-	-
16. C	-	-	-	-	-	-	-	-	Јј	j	-
17. C	Кк	k	Кк	k	Кк	k	Кк	k	Кк	k	Ққ Ӄӄ
18. C	Лл	l	Лл	l	Лл	l	Лл	l	Лл	l	Љљ
19. C	-	-	-	-	-	-	-	-	Љљ	lj	-
20. C	Мм	m	Мм	m	Мм	m	Мм	m	Мм	m	-
21. C	Нн	n	Нн	n	Нн	n	Нн	n	Нн	n	Ӈӈ Ҥҥ Ңң
22. C	-	-	-	-	-	-	-	-	Њњ	nj	-
23. N	Оо	o	Оо	o	Оо	o	Оо	o	Оо	o	Ӧӧ Ѳѳ Ӫ
24. C	Пп	p	Пп	p	Пп	p	Пп	p	Пп	p	-
25. C	Рр	r	Рр	r	Рр	r	Рр	r	Рр	r	-
26. C	Сс	s	Сс	s	Сс	s	Сс	s	Сс	s	Ҫҫ
27. C	Тт	t	Тт	t	Тт	t	Тт	t	Тт	t	Тт
28 C	-	-	-	-	-	-	-	-	Ћћ	ć	-
29. N	Уу	u	Уу	u	Уу	u	Уу	u	Уу	u	Ӳӳ Ӱӱ Ўў Үү Ұ
30. C	-	-	-	-	Ўў	w	-	-	-	-	Үү Vv Ѵѵ
31. C	Фф	f	Фф	f	Фф	f	Фф	f	Фф	f	-
32. C	Хх	kh	Хх	kh	Хх	kh	Хх	kh	Хх	h	Хх
33. C	Цц	ts	Цц	ts	Цц	ts	Цц	ts	Цц	c	-
34. C	Чч	ch	Чч	ch	Чч	ch	Чч	ch	Чч	č	Ҷҷ Ӌӌ Ҹҹ
35. C	-	-	-	-	-	-	-	-	Џџ	dž	hh
36. C	Шш	sh	Шш	sh	Шш	sh	Шш	sh	Шш	š	-
37. C	Щщ	shch	Щщ	shch	-	-	Щщ	sht	-	-	-
38. N	Ъъ	"	-	-	-	-	Ъъ	ŭ	-	-	-
39. N	Ыы	y	-	-	Ыы	y	-	-	-	-	-
40. N	Ьь	'	Ьь	'	Ьь	'	Ьь	'	-	-	Ыы
41. N	Ээ	e	-	-	Ээ	e	-	-	-	-	-
42. N	Юю	yu	Юю	yu	Юю	yu	Юю	yu	-	-	-
43. N	Яя	ya	Яя	ya	Яя	ya	Яя	ya	-	-	-

Figure D-3. Cyrillic Alphabet and Transliteration Chart

FM 2-22.401/NTTP 2-01.4/AFTTP(I) 3-2.63   **9 June 2006**

NOTES:
1. The letters are numbered sequentially for ease of reference. The alphabetic order given is the convenient one, which is not necessarily the traditional one.
2. The letters marked "N" are nonconsonants; and the letters marked "C" are consonants.
3. Letters 7 and 8 have alternate transliterations for Russian and Belorussian. In all cases, the first transliteration is used when the letter occurs after a "C" letter; the second transliteration is used in all other cases, including when the letter begins the word.
4. Letter 8 is not considered a separate letter and its dieresis is often omitted.
5. Letter 4 is pronounced something like "h" in Ukrainian and Belorussian and "h" is often the recommended transliteration. However, transliteration "g" is recommended here to eliminate confusion with the letters transliterated "sh" and "zh."
6. The "Other" category refers to various minority languages in the Soviet Union, many of which are Uralic or Altaic languages.

Figure D-3. Cyrillic Alphabet and Transliteration Chart (continued).

UKRAINIAN: Ukrainian is distinguished by the use of letters 12 and 13 and the non-use of letter 39. Letters 9 and 14 also are unique to Ukrainian, but their frequency is low and their absence may be accidental. When Ukrainian is identified, pay particular attention to the transliteration of letter 12. The recommended transliteration for letter 4 is "g" even though its pronunciation is closer to English "h."

BELORUSSIAN: Belorussian is distinguished by the use of letters 13 and 39 and the non-use of letter 12. Letter 30 is unique to Belorussian, but its frequency is not high enough to use it as an identification sign. As in Ukrainian, letter 4 in Belorussian is transliterated "g" and pronounced like "h."

SERBIAN: Serbian is spotted easily by the several unique letters it uses: letters 6, 16, 19, 22, 28, and 35. Serbian is conventionally transliterated into Croatian, and this is what the chart gives. The diacritics of the Croatian script are discussed in the **"ROMAN ALPHABET LANGUAGES"** section above.

MACEDONIAN: Macedonian is spoken by perhaps two million people in southeastern Yugoslavia. The Macedonian alphabet is similar to the Serbian, except that letters 6 and 28 are not used and three other letters are added.

ARABIC ALPHABET LANGUAGES

The Arabic alphabet has generally followed the spread of Islam and has been used to write numerous languages, some of which (notably Turkish) no longer use it. This alphabet, appropriately modified, currently is used for all the dialects of Arabic and for Persian, Urdu, and other Indo-Iranian languages, such as Dari, Pashto, and Kurdish. The Russian and Cyrillic alphabets seem even more related to one another when compared to Arabic.

ARABIC AND PERSIAN: The best distinction a nonlinguist can make is to separate Persian documents from Arabic documents. Persian linguists cannot read Arabic, and vice versa, unless they know both languages.

ARABIC: Arabic is spoken over a large area extending from Morocco on the west to borders of ancient Persia (modern Iran) on the east. The spoken language varies widely in this area, but the written language is fairly standard. Only a specialist could hope to distinguish the varieties of Arabic, but a sharp-eyed nonlinguist can learn to recognize Arabic and distinguish it from Persian. The best indication is perhaps the presence of letter 32, which is not used in Persian. A final characteristic is the absence of the special Persian letters: letters 3, 7, 14, and 26. Since this is a negative indication, however, it cannot be used by itself to prove that a text is Arabic.

PERSIAN: Persian is used in Iran. It is indicated by the presence of the special Persian letters 3, 7, 14, and 26, and by the absence of letter 32. Other indications are a paucity of letter 1 and 27 combinations (the Arabic definite article) and a slightly different preference in numeral usage.

ARABIC NUMERALS: In school, the numerals used in the United States and most of the rest of the world are often called "Arabic numerals," but these are not the same forms used in Arabic alphabet languages. The real Arabic numerals are illustrated in Figure D-4. This figure also shows Arabic and Persian variants of the numerals along with their international equivalents. Unlike the Arabic alphabet (which is, of course, read from right to left), ARABIC NUMERALS ARE READ FROM LEFT TO RIGHT, THE SAME WAY AS OUR OWN NUMERALS ARE READ.

International	Arabic	Persian	International	Arabic	Persian
0	٠	٥ or ٠	6	٦	۶ or ٦
1	١	١	7	٧	٧
2	٢	٢	8	٨	٨
3	٣	٣	9	٩	٩
4	٤	۴ or ٤	10	١٠	١٥ or ١٠
5	٥	۵ or ٥	20	٢٠	٢٥ or ٢٠

Figure D-4. International, Arabic, and Persian Numbers

Document collectors should familiarize themselves with the Arabic numerals so they can read page numbers in collected documents and properly reassemble documents that have come apart. Collectors should remember that one of the results of the right-to-left orientation of the Arabic alphabet is that the apparent "back" of a document is actually the front.

Figure D-5 illustrates the Arabic alphabet in its Arabic and Persian variants. Notice that each letter has four forms, labeled "alone," "final," "medial," and "initial." Notice that "initial" is to the right of "final." These column labels indicate two of the main differences between

Arabic script and Roman script: First, the letters change in order to connect to other letters, and second, **THE SCRIPT IS WRITTEN FROM RIGHT TO LEFT.** The letters with asterisks by their numbers cannot connect to a following letter. The initial form is used to begin a word or when the letter follows a nonconnectable letter. The medial form is used after a connectable letter or when it is used by itself; for example, to letter paragraphs in a document.

No.	Arabic				Persian			
	Alone	Final	Medial	Initial	Alone	Final	Medial	Initial
1.	ا	ﺎ	ﺎ	ا	ا	ﺎ	ﺎ	ا
2.	ب	ﺐ	ﺒ	ﺑ	ب	ﺐ	ﺒ	ﺑ
3.	-	-	-	-	پ	ﭗ	ﭙ	ﭘ
4.	ت	ﺖ	ﺘ	ﺗ	ت	ﺖ	ﺘ	ﺗ
5.	ث	ﺚ	ﺜ	ﺛ	ث	ﺚ	ﺜ	ﺛ
6.	ج	ﺞ	ﺠ	ﺟ	ج	ﺞ	ﺠ	ﺟ
7.	-	-	-	-	چ	ﭻ	ﭽ	ﭼ
8.	ح	ﺢ	ﺤ	ﺣ	ح	ﺢ	ﺤ	ﺣ
9.	خ	ﺦ	ﺨ	ﺧ	خ	ﺦ	ﺨ	ﺧ
10.	د	ﺪ	ﺪ	د	د	ﺪ	ﺪ	د
11.	ذ	ﺬ	ﺬ	ذ	ذ	ﺬ	ﺬ	ذ
12.	ر	ﺮ	ﺮ	ر	ر	ﺮ	ﺮ	ر
13.	ز	ﺰ	ﺰ	ز	ز	ﺰ	ﺰ	ز
14.	-	-	-	-	ژ	ﮋ	ﮋ	ژ
15.	س	ﺲ	ﺴ	ﺳ	س	ﺲ	ﺴ	ﺳ
16.	ش	ﺶ	ﺸ	ﺷ	ش	ﺶ	ﺸ	ﺷ
17.	ص	ﺺ	ﺼ	ﺻ	ص	ﺺ	ﺼ	ﺻ
18.	ض	ﺾ	ﻀ	ﺿ	ض	ﺾ	ﻀ	ﺿ
19.	ط	ﻂ	ﻄ	ﻃ	ط	ﻂ	ﻄ	ﻃ
20.	ظ	ﻆ	ﻈ	ﻇ	ظ	ﻆ	ﻈ	ﻇ
21.	ع	ﻊ	ﻌ	ﻋ	ع	ﻊ	ﻌ	ﻋ
22.	غ	ﻎ	ﻐ	ﻏ	غ	ﻎ	ﻐ	ﻏ
23.	ف	ﻒ	ﻔ	ﻓ	ف	ﻒ	ﻔ	ﻓ
24.	ق	ﻖ	ﻘ	ﻗ	ق	ﻖ	ﻘ	ﻗ
25.	ك	ﻚ	ﻜ	ﻛ	ك	ﻚ	ﻜ	ﻛ
26.	-	-	-	-	گ	ﮓ	ﮕ	ﮔ
27.	ل	ﻞ	ﻠ	ﻟ	ل	ﻞ	ﻠ	ﻟ
28.	م	ﻢ	ﻤ	ﻣ	م	ﻢ	ﻤ	ﻣ
29.	ن	ﻦ	ﻨ	ﻧ	ن	ﻦ	ﻨ	ﻧ
30.	و	ﻮ	ﻮ	و	و	ﻮ	ﻮ	و
31.	ه	ﻪ	ﻬ	ﻫ	ه	ﻪ	ﻬ	ﻫ
32.	ة	ﺔ	-	-	-	-	-	-
33.	ي	ﻲ	ﻴ	ﻳ	ی	ﯽ	ﯿ	ﯾ

Figure D-5. The Arabic Alphabet

DIACRITICS: Another feature of the Arabic alphabet is the use of diacritics to differentiate many of the letters. Figure D-6 illustrates the diacritics used in Arabic and Persian.

< ˙ >	High Dot	< ˙˙ >	High Double Dot	< ⸚ >	High Triple Dot
< ˏ >	Low Dot	< ˏˏ >	Low Double Dot	< ⸰ >	Low Triple Dot
< ˉ >	Flag High	< ⁼ >	Double Flag High	< ر >	Hamza Sign Persian
< ͜ >	Flag Low	< ⸗ >	Double Flag Low	< ء >	Hamza Sign Arabic

Figure D-6. The Diacritics of Arabic and Persian

SAMPLES OF ARABIC AND PERSIAN

Figure D-7 gives a sample of printed Arabic. Note the frequent occurrences of letter 1 and letter 27: the definite article at word beginnings. Remember, words begin on the right. The seventh line from the top, for instance, has four obvious occurrences and two other occurrences in modified forms that have not been discussed here. There are 18 occurrences of letter 32, at least one occurrence in every line except lines 9 and 11 and four occurrences in lines 3 and 8.

وفضــلا عن ذلك فلقد كان فى كل القوانين القائمة ما يكفى لمواجهة الأحداث
والاضطرابات التى وقعت وكذلك للنظر فى أمر ما نـسب رئيس الجمهورية فى خطابه إلى
أحزاب الأقلية ، وإلى الجماعات الإسلامية ،. وإلى بعض الشخصيات المدنية المسلمة ،
والمسيحية .. فالقـوانين القائمة تكفل الحفاظ على أمن البلاد وسـلامتها ضـد ما يهدد
وحدتها الوطنية من أخطار وبالتالى فان القرار المطعون فيه لايمكن أن يعتبر ـ بحال ـ
عملا من أعمال الضرورة ـ كما أن القرار المطعون فيه خالف صريح نص المادة ٤١ من
الدستور التى تنص على عدم جواز القبض أو تقييد الحريات فى غير حالة التلبس إلا
بأمر من القـاضى المختص أو النيابة العامة ، تـستلزمه ضرورةالتحقيق وصيانة أمن
المجتمع وفقا لأحكام القانون ـ وأنه لم يرد فى أوراق الدعوى أى دليل على أن المتحفظ
عليهم ضبطوا فى حالة تلبس أو أنه أجرى معهم تحقيق سابق على التحفظ ، حتى يتضح
منه أن هذا التحفظ كان اجراء لازما .

Figure D-7. Printed Arabic

Figure D-8 illustrates typewritten Arabic. Note that lines 1, 2 5, and 10 begin (on the right) with the definite article (letter 1 and letter 27). There are 20 other obvious occurrences of these letters at the beginning of words and several others that are less obvious. Lines 1, 2, and 9 end (on the left) with letter 32. Letter 32 occurs five other times in the sample. Arabic script permits some letters to be stretched in order to even out text on the left. The long lines at the left of the sample are instances of this.

الدفع ببطلان اجراءات التحقيق لعدم توفير حماية
التحقيق الابتدائي وهو حق المتهم في الاستعانة
بمحام - اعمالا لنص المادتين ٦٩ / ٧١ من الدستور
والمواد ٧٧ - ١٢٤ - ١٢٥ من قانون الاجراءات
الجنائية وأنه لا يقدح من ذلك أن المتهمين لم يودعوا
تقريرا في قلم كتاب المحكمة بأسماء محاميهم وذلك
لان ظروف المتهمين والحالة التي كانوا عليها قبل
عرضهم على النيابة العامة كانت لا تسمح لهم بايداع
تقرير في قلم كتاب المحكمة بأسماء محاميهم وأن العبارة
التي يثبتها المحقق في صور محضر التحقيق من أنه
سأل المتهم عما اذا كان لديه محام تنفي ذلك - وهي

Figure D-8. Typewritten Arabic

Figure D-9 illustrates printed Persian. Note the double flags, two in the first line and eight more in the rest of the sample. Note the low triple dots, one in the first line and eight more in the rest of the sample. Neither of these diacritics occurs in Arabic.

بعد از شاه عباس بزرگ در سال ١٠٣٨ کمپانی تجارتی هند شرقی انگلیس فرمان
تازه در باب تجارت ابریشم از شاه صفی جانشین وی گرفتند ولی نتوانستند تمام
امتیازات و حقوق را که در زمان شاه عباس بزرگ تحصیل کرده بودند بار دیگر
بدست آورند و با آنکه از طرف چارلز اول پادشاه انگلیس در ماه شعبان ١٠٣٩
(١٦٣٠) نماینده و نامه برای کمک و مساعدت بتجار و اتباع انگلیسی در ایران
برای شاه صفی آمد و از طرف پادشاه ایران هم بخوبی این اظهار مودت و دوستی
پذیرفته شد ولی در زمان این پادشاه اساساً قسمت مهم تجارت ایران بدست تجار
هلندی بود و بار دیگر چارلز اول برای کمک بشرکت هند شرقی انگلیس نامه
دیگر برای شاه صفی فرستاد و از طرف پادشاه صفوی هم این نامه بخوبی پذیرفته

Figure D-9. Printed Persian (Arrows indicate distinguishing features.)

OTHER ARABIC ALPHABET LANGUAGES

DARI: Dari is used in Afghanistan and favored by the government. Since its written form is heavily influenced by Persian models, there is no easy way for the nonspecialist to distinguish it from Persian.

KURDISH, PASHTO, AND URDU: The other notable Arabic alphabet languages are Kurdish, Pashto, and Urdu. Kurdish is spoken by the Kurdish tribes of Iraq, Iran, and Turkey. Pashto is used widely in Afghanistan, and Urdu is the predominant language of Pakistan. These languages contain letters and diacritics not listed for Arabic or Persian. If one of these languages is suspected, refer the problem to a linguist.

CHARACTER LANGUAGES

Character languages use writing systems with symbols that stand for words or meaningful elements of words rather than for sounds. Character languages, such as hieroglyphic Egyptian, existed in earlier times; but today, the only character languages are Chinese and languages that have wholly or partially borrowed the Chinese system, such as Japanese and Korean.

DISTINGUISHING CHINESE, JAPANESE, AND KOREAN

The easy way to distinguish the three languages is to look for the distinctive phonetic symbols of Japanese and Korean. If these symbols are not present, conclude that the language is Chinese. Chinese is the model for the other two, and these languages borrow freely from Chinese. Figures D-10, D-11, and D-12 give sample texts of Chinese, Japanese, and Korean.

Figure D-10 shows Chinese characters. They are more detailed, complex, and square or precise than Japanese or Korean. Korean and Japanese language texts use Chinese characters whenever it might be unclear to use one of their own symbols. This means that the higher or more academic a text is the more Chinese characters it will have.

出 版 说 明

《汉英词典》是由北京外国语学院英语系编写的。编写工作于一九七一年开始，一九七八年夏完成，历时八载。先后参加编写、修改等工作的中外专家共五十余人。

本书的主编为北京外国语学院英语系系主任吴景荣教授。除编写组编辑人员外，还有不少专家和学者先后参加过这项工作。周珏良主持了初稿的编写，弗兰克·怀利（Frank Wylie）和何兰蕙（Nancy Hodes）参加了英语修改工作。在组内工作了较长时间的还有初大告、水天同、王锡钧、张道真、王瑞、俞天民、吴国瑞、杨志才、吴石牧、陈国成、张月平等。在词典编写过程中，还得到丘茉莉（Elsie Fairfax-Cholmeley）、舒裕禄（Norman Shulman）和裘克安等对本书的编辑和出版提出了许多宝贵的意见。

本书是一部中型语文工具书，全书收汉语单字条目六千多，其中包括极少数的音变字，收入的多字条目五万余，连同合成词、词化短语、及例证等共达十二万余。

除一般词语外，还收一些常见的文言词语、方言、成语、谚语，以及自然科学和社会科学的常用词语。

Figure D-10. Sample of Chinese Text

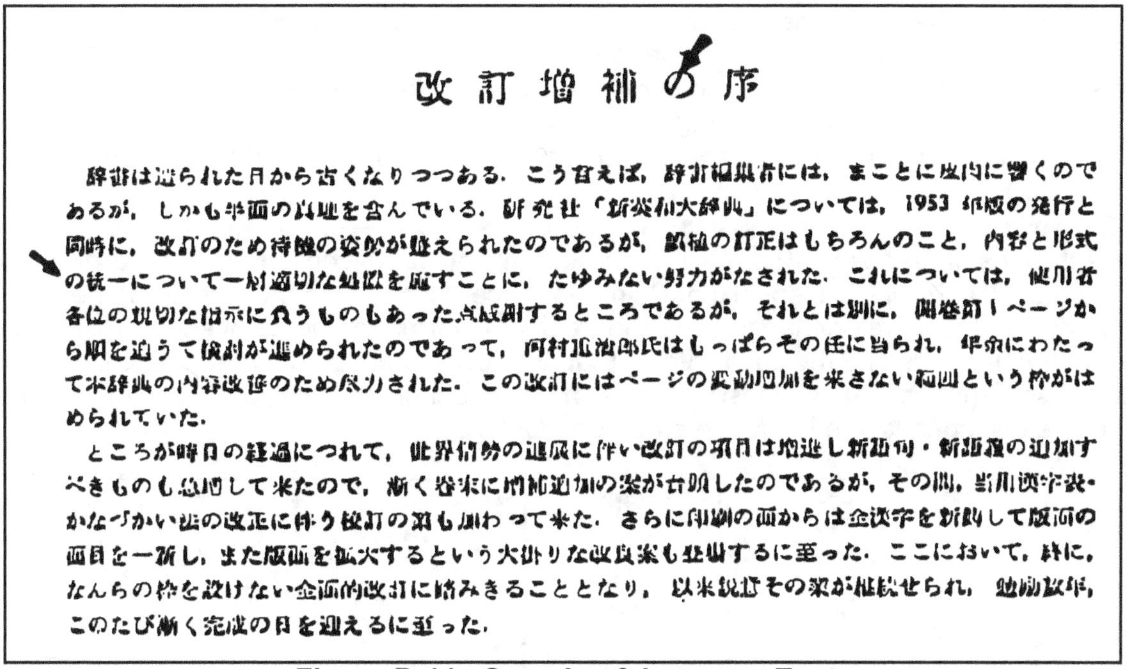

改訂増補の序

辞書は造られた日から古くなりつつある．こう言えば，辞書編集者には，まことに身内に響くのであるが，しかも半面の真理を含んでいる．研究社「新和英大辞典」については，1953年版の発行と同時に，改訂のため待機の姿勢が整えられたのであるが，誤植の訂正はもちろんのこと，内容と形式の統一について一層適切な処置を施すことに，たゆみない努力がなされた．これについては，使用者各位の親切な指示に負うものもあった点感謝するところであるが，それとは別に，開巻第1ページから順を追うて検討が進められたのであって，河村重治郎氏はもっぱらその任に当られ，年余にわたって本辞典の内容改善のため尽力された．この改訂にはページの変動増加を来さない範囲という枠がはめられていた．

ところが時日の経過につれて，世界情勢の進展に伴い改訂の項目は増進し新語句・新語義の追加すべきものも急増して来たので，漸く巻末に増補追加の案が台頭したのであるが，その間，当用漢字表・かなづかい法の改正に伴う校訂の案も加わって来た．さらに印刷の面からは全活字を新鋳して版面の面目を一新し，また版面を拡大するという大掛りな改良案も提出するに至った．ここにおいて，遂に，なんらの枠を設けない全面的改訂に踏みきることとなり，以来設計その案が推敲せられ，勉励数年，このたび漸く完成の日を迎えるに至った．

Figure D-11. Sample of Japanese Text

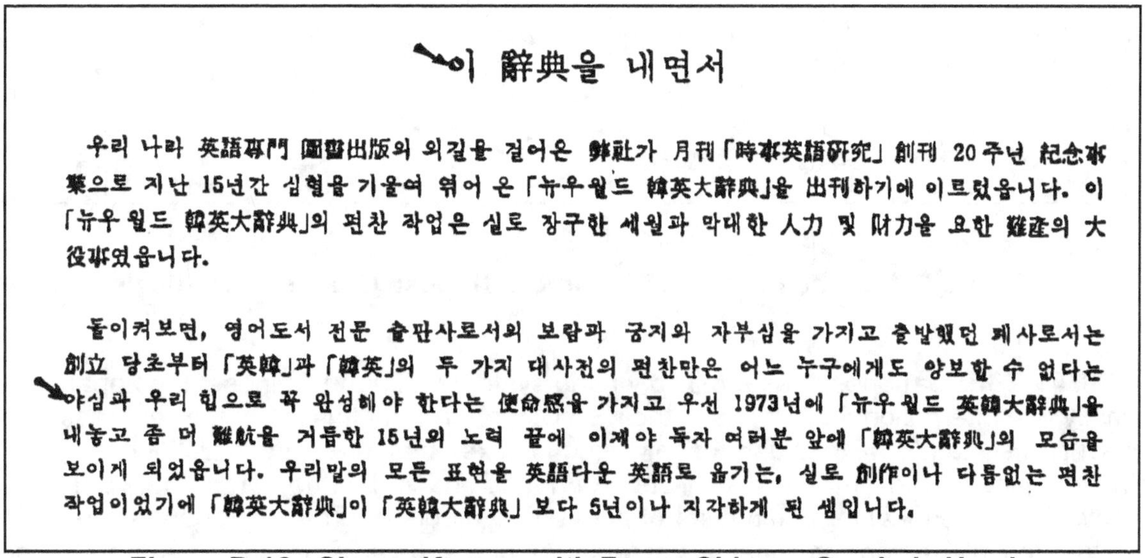

이 辭典을 내면서

우리 나라 英語專門 圖書出版의 외길을 걸어온 弊社가 月刊「時事英語研究」創刊 20주년 紀念事業으로 지난 15년간 심혈을 기울여 엮어 온「뉴우월드 韓英大辭典」을 出刊하기에 이르렀읍니다. 이「뉴우월드 韓英大辭典」의 편찬 작업은 실로 장구한 세월과 막대한 人力 및 財力을 요한 難産의 大役事였읍니다.

돌이켜보면, 영어도서 전문 출판사로서의 보람과 긍지와 자부심을 가지고 출발했던 폐사로서는 創立 당초부터「英韓」과「韓英」의 두 가지 대사전의 편찬만은 어느 누구에게도 양보할 수 없다는 야심과 우리 힘으로 꼭 완성해야 한다는 使命感을 가지고 우선 1973년에「뉴우월드 英韓大辭典」을 내놓고 좀 더 難航을 거듭한 15년의 노력 끝에 이제야 독자 여러분 앞에「韓英大辭典」의 모습을 보이게 되었읍니다. 우리말의 모든 표현을 英語다운 英語로 옮기는, 실로 創作이나 다름없는 편찬 작업이었기에「韓英大辭典」이「英韓大辭典」보다 5년이나 지각하게 된 셈입니다.

Figure D-12. Shows Korean with Fewer Chinese Symbols Used

NOTE: North Korean text seldom has any Chinese characters as a matter of official policy.

CHINESE: Chinese is written with several thousand symbols called characters. International numerals are widely used and scientific and technical Chinese will contain quoted European words in Roman letters. The characters are constructed according to a complex system based on the use of only a few different stroke types (less than 10) and a large set of elements called "radicals" (about 200). Radicals are made up of one or more elements associated with them. These radicals and strokes are used to construct the characters. The characters are thought of as occupying a rectangular space and good calligraphy allots about the same area to each character, regardless of complexity.

Figure D-13 shows the 50 most common radicals in Chinese. Some will occur by themselves as characters. Most will more frequently occur as constituents of more complex characters. The People's Republic of China has recently changed the form of some of these elements, but most are unchanged and the traditional forms still occur even there. Except for numerical zeroes and the small circles that are used as punctuation marks to indicate the end of a sentence, printed Chinese does not have any circles. If the text has a lot of circles and curves, suspect some language other than Chinese.

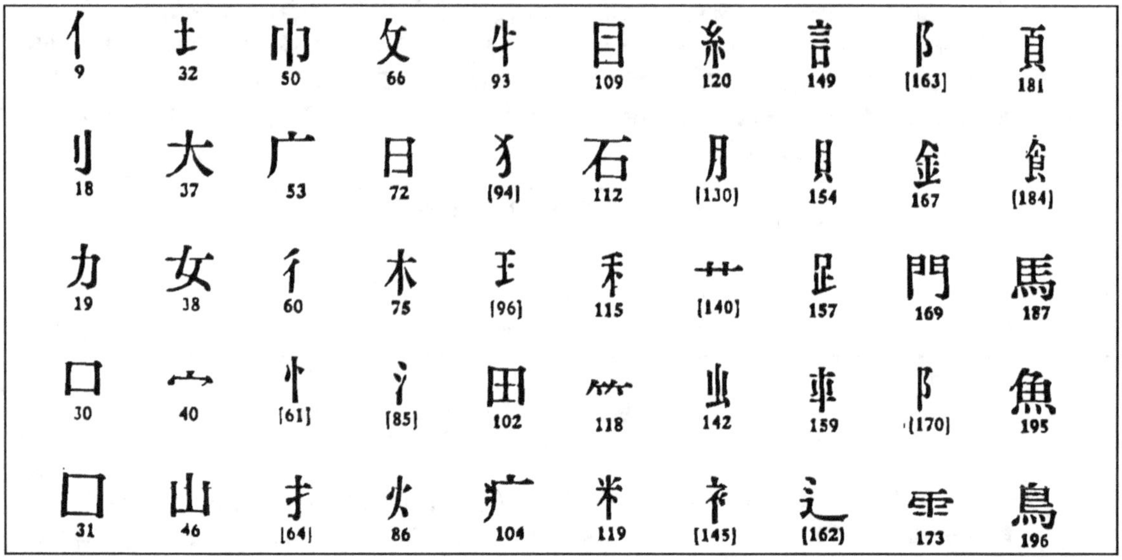

Figure D-13. The Fifty Most Common Chinese Character Radicals

JAPANESE: Japanese has a mixed writing system. Like the Chinese, the Japanese normally use international numerals in their S&T literature; but this is not the real reason their writing system is mixed. Japanese writing is mixed because, in general, it uses Chinese characters to write the lexical stem of nouns and verbs (the part of the word that conveys the basic meaning); and a set of phonetic symbols invented in Japan called **hiragana** to write the grammatical affixes of the nouns and verbs as well as entire auxiliary words.

Japanese also use another set of phonetic symbols, also invented in Japan, called **katakana** to write words borrowed from European languages. The presence of these katakana symbols distinguishes Japanese. Normal prose will contain perhaps 60 to 70 percent hiragana symbols. Unlike Chinese characters, hiragana are written with curved strokes. Katakana are less frequent.

The hiragana are illustrated in Figure D-14 and the katakana are illustrated in Figure D-15. Pay particular attention to the fifth symbol from the left in the bottom row of the hiragana

(Figure D-14), the one labeled "no." This symbol is used to write a very common grammatical affix. It will almost always occur frequently in any Japanese text.

あ a	か ka	さ sa	た ta	な na	は ha	ま ma	や ya	ら ra	わ wa	
い i	き ki	し shi	ち chi	に ni	ひ hi	み mi	い (y)i	り ri	ゐ wi	
う u	く ku	す su	つ tsu	ぬ nu	ふ fu	む mu	ゆ yu	る ru	う (w)u	
え e	け ke	せ se	て te	ね ne	へ he	め me	え (y)e	れ re	ゑ (w)e	
お o	こ ko	そ so	と to	の no	ほ ho	も mo	よ yo	ろ ro	を (w)o	ん n

Figure D-14. The Japanese Hiragana Syllabary

ア a	カ ka	サ sa	タ ta	ナ na	ハ ha	マ ma	ヤ ya	ラ ra	ワ wa	
イ i	キ ki	シ shi	チ chi	ニ ni	ヒ hi	ミ mi	イ (y)i	リ ri	ヰ (w)i	
ウ u	ク ku	ス su	ツ tsu	ヌ nu	フ fu	ム mu	ユ yu	ル ru	ウ (w)u	
エ e	ケ ke	セ se	テ te	ネ ne	ヘ he	メ me	エ (y)e	レ re	エ (w)e	
オ o	コ ko	ソ so	ト to	ノ no	ホ ho	モ mo	ヨ yo	ロ ro	ヲ (w)o	ン n

Figure D-15. The Japanese Katakana Syllabary

KOREAN: Korean can be written entirely in its native alphabet. Therefore, symbols from this script will overwhelmingly predominate in any normal Korean text. Chinese characters, however, are considered learned and prestigious, so a certain number of them will be encountered in quantities that vary with the pretensions of the author.

The Korean alphabet was developed under the influence of Chinese writing models, so to the untrained eye Korean alphabetic writing looks like Chinese characters. The letters of European alphabets form words, but the symbols of the Korean alphabet are grouped together to form a syllable. This means that a Korean word may extend over several groupings. Also, while the letters of European words are read horizontally, Korean alphabetic symbols are read vertically—from the top to the bottom of each group—with the left preceding the right when the symbols are side-by-side. Figure D-16 illustrates the symbols of the Korean alphabet. Pay close attention to the second symbol from the left in the third row, the one that looks like a circle with a stem at the 12 o'clock position. It is a very frequent symbol and does not look like anything that occurs in Chinese or Japanese.

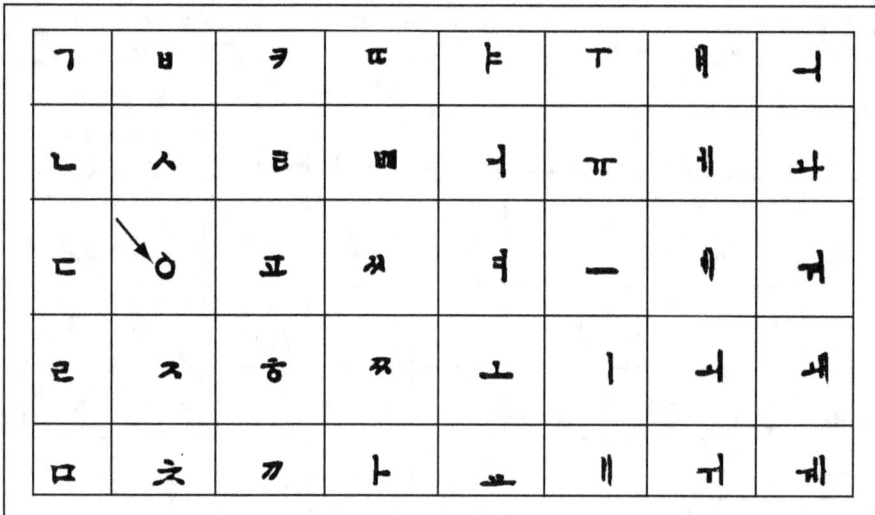

Figure D-16. The Korean Alphabet

Appendix E

MARKING AND TAGGING

Labeling CEM properly is vital to the timely exploitation of the item. It speeds up the often slow process of producing effective countermeasures for the Soldier in combat. Proper labeling provides the analyst information necessary for the item's timely exploitation. It also allows interrogators and TECHINT elements to match up knowledgeable prisoners with the CEM from which they became separated in the evacuation process.

Responsibilities:

The capturing unit is responsible for properly marking and tagging CEM. The responsibilities must be clearly established by command SOP. The equipment and document tags accompany the materiel to its final destination. As part of core training, all personnel should be instructed on how to tag CEM. They should know the consequences when personnel and equipment are not properly tagged. Training should stress protecting and preserving the original markings on materiel at the time of capture. Weather-resistant capture tags are used. They are securely attached to the item itself and to the shipping container. If weather-resistant tags are not available, use any material (for example, rations packing) on which pertinent capture data can be recorded.

There are two procedures for marking and tagging CEM. The procedure used depends on whether or not the captured item is associated with a captured person.

CEM with EPWs:

For CEM with personnel, tag the captured person and any associated CEM with the three-part EPW tag (DD Form 2745). An example of this tag is at Figure E-1.

CEM by Itself:

For CEM by itself, tag the piece of equipment and associated document with part C of the EPW capture tag. In addition, label all documents believed to be of a technical nature (such as operator manuals) with the flag word "TECHDOC."

Part A (front)

1. DATE AND TIME OF CAPTURE		2. SERIAL NO.		**A**
3. NAME			4. DATE OF BIRTH	
5. RANK		6. SERVICE NO.		
7. UNIT OF EPW		8. CAPTURING UNIT		
9. LOCATION OF CAPTURE *(Grid coordinates)*				
10. CIRCUMSTANCES OF CAPTURE	11. PHYSICAL CONDITION OF EPW	12. WEAPONS, EQUIPMENT, DOCUMENTS		

DD FORM 2745, MAY 96   REPLACES DA FORM 5976, JAN 91, USABLE UNTIL EXHAUSTED.

Part A (back)

ENEMY PRISONER OF WAR (EPW) CAPTURE TAG (PART A)

For use of this form, see AR 190-8.
The proponent agency is DCSOPS.

Attach this part of tag to EPW. *(Do not remove from EPW.)*

1. **Search** - For weapons, military documents, or special equipment.
2. **Silence** - Prohibit talking among EPWs for ease of control.
3. **Segregate** - By rank, sex, and nationality.
4. **Safeguard** - To prevent harm or escape.
5. **Speed** - Evacuate from the combat zone.
6. **Tag** - Prisoners and documents or special equipment.

DD FORM 2745 (BACK), MAY 96

Part B (front)

1. DATE AND TIME OF CAPTURE		2. SERIAL NO.		**B**
3. NAME			4. DATE OF BIRTH	
5. RANK		6. SERVICE NO.		
7. UNIT OF EPW		8. CAPTURING UNIT		
9. LOCATION OF CAPTURE *(Grid coordinates)*				
10. CIRCUMSTANCES OF CAPTURE	11. PHYSICAL CONDITION OF EPW	12. WEAPONS, EQUIPMENT, DOCUMENTS		

DD FORM 2745, MAY 96   REPLACES DA FORM 5976, JAN 91, USABLE UNTIL EXHAUSTED.

Part B (back)

UNIT RECORD CARD (PART B)

Forward to Unit.

(Capturing unit retains for records.)

Use string, wire, or other durable material to attach the appropriate section of this form to the EPW's equipment or property.

DD FORM 2745 (BACK), MAY 96

Part C (front)

1. DATE AND TIME OF CAPTURE		2. SERIAL NO.		**C**
3. NAME			4. DATE OF BIRTH	
5. RANK		6. SERVICE NO.		
7. UNIT OF EPW		8. CAPTURING UNIT		
9. LOCATION OF CAPTURE *(Grid coordinates)*				
10. DESCRIPTION OF WEAPONS, SPECIAL EQUIPMENT, DOCUMENTS				

DD FORM 2745, MAY 96   REPLACES DA FORM 5976, JAN 91, USABLE UNTIL EXHAUSTED

Part C (back)

DOCUMENT/SPECIAL EQUIPMENT WEAPONS CARD (PART C)

Attach this part of tag to property taken. *(Do not remove from property.)*

As a minimum, the tag must include the following information:

Item 1. Date and time of capture *(YYYYMMDD)*.
Item 8. Capturing unit.
Item 9. Place of capture *(grid coordinates)*.
Item 10. Circumstances of capture *(how the EPW was captured)*.

DD FORM 2745 (BACK), MAY 96

Figure E-1. Example of the Front and Reverse Sides of an EPW Capture Tag (DD Form 2745)

E-2   FM 2-22.401/NTTP 2-01.4/AFTTP(I) 3-2.63   9 June 2006

Appendix F

MOVEMENT AND STORAGE OF CAPTURED MATERIEL

References:

AFMAN 24-204 (I)/TM 38-250/NAVSUP PUB 505/MCO P4030.19H/DLAI 4145.3, *Preparing Hazardous Materials for Military Air Shipments*
USDOT, Transportation—Code of Federal Regulations (CFR) Title 49 Parts 100-185, *Hazardous Materials Regulations*
International Air Transport Association (IATA). See their website http://www.iata.org for additional information.
TM 60A 1-1-22, *EOD Procedures /General EOD Safety Procedures*
DOD 6055.9-STD, *DOD Ammunition and Explosives Safety Standards*
DA PAM 385-64, *Ammunition and Explosives Safety Standards*
AR 190-11, *Physical Security of Arms, Ammunition, and Explosives*

Purpose: Assist in the decision making process pertaining to transportation and storage of captured materiel (CM).

General: Transportation and storage of CM can involve serious hazards and risks to personnel and facilities. This appendix provides reference materials to aid in the safe movement and storage of CM. Figure F-1 provides a decision matrix to evaluate CM for transport from the point of capture to the storage center. Figure F-2 provides a decision matrix to evaluate CM for proper storage at the storage center. Figure F-3 provides a decision matrix to evaluate CM for transport from the storage center to CONUS.

Storage Center: Storage areas must be provided for non-hazardous CM, hazardous (non-explosive) CM, and explosive CM. Explosive CM will be stored in an ammunition holding area (AHA). Design and operation of the AHA must be IAW applicable regulations and publications (DOD 6055.9-STD).

AHAs have specific limits set for Net Explosive Weight (NEW) and the type of explosives that can be stored. (See DA PAM 385-64.) DA PAM 385-64 also provides guidance regarding the compatibility for storage of various classes and types of explosives.

Storing hazardous CM may involve various chemicals, batteries, or other hazardous materiel. The Code of Federal Regulations, Title 49 Parts 100 to 185 can be used as a guideline to determine if an item is hazardous, and what precautions must be taken to safely handle possible hazards. Measures must be taken to protect all CM from adverse environmental conditions.

All personnel involved are responsible for ensuring that the transportation and storage of CM is carried out in a safe and prudent manner. Anyone that becomes aware of an unsafe condition will immediately notify all personnel at risk and take appropriate corrective action to mitigate the hazard.

Note: SAFETY IS PRIORITY NUMBER 1 WHEN TRANSPORTING AND STORING CAPTURED MATERIEL.

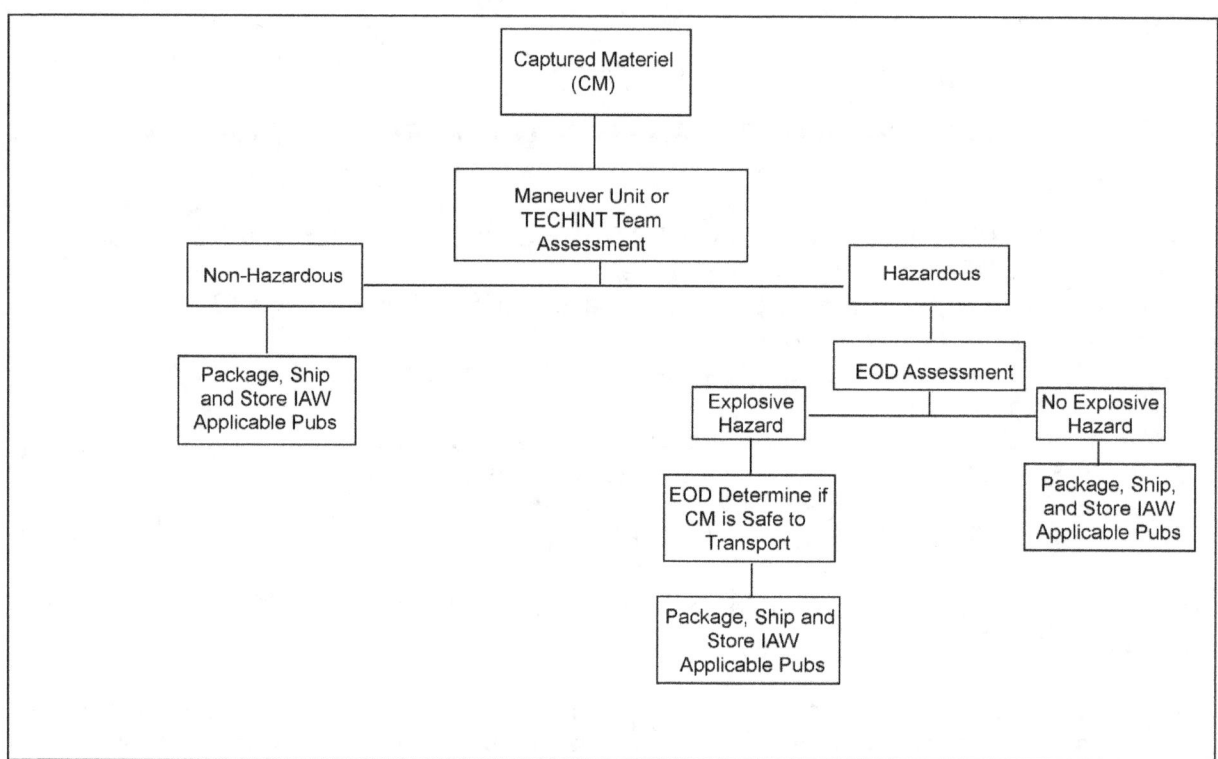

Figure F-1. Movement of Captured Materiel from Collection Point to Storage

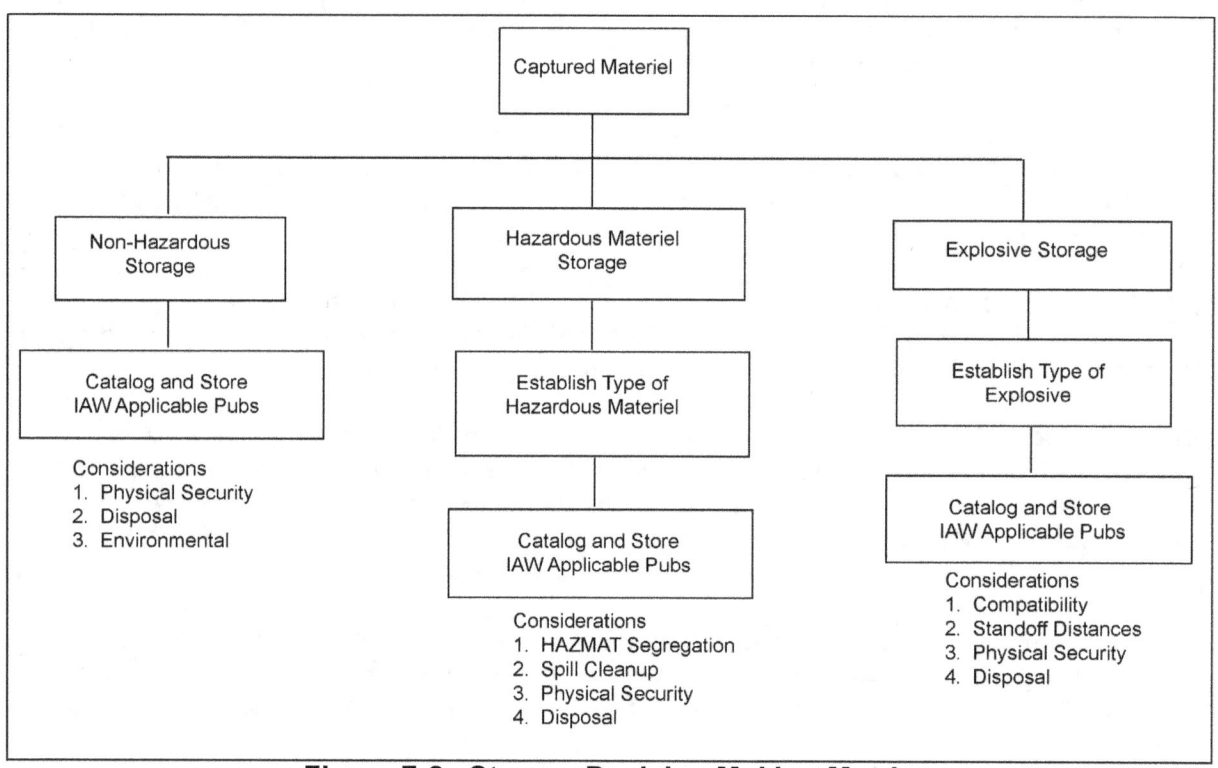

Figure F-2. Storage Decision Making Matrix

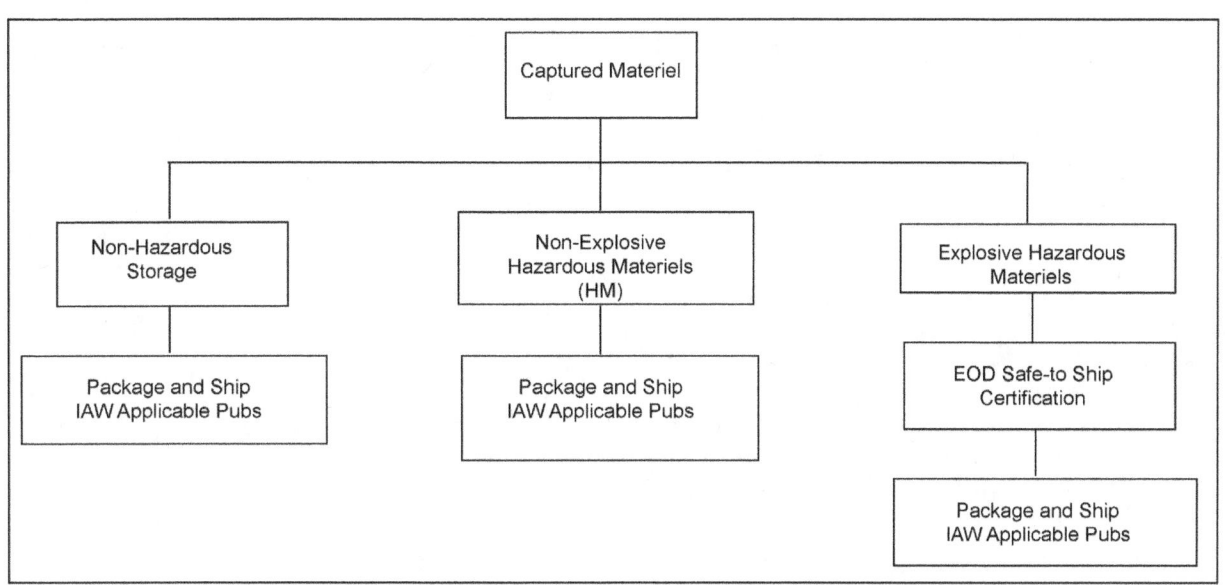

Figure F-3. Shipment to CONUS Decision Matrix

This page intentionally left blank.

REFERENCES

Joint
NATO STANAG 2084, *Handling and Reporting of Captured Enemy Equipment and Documents,* Edition No. 6, May 1999

Army
AR 190-8, *Enemy Prisoners of War, Retained Personnel, Civilian Internees and Other Detainees*
AR 190-11, *Physical Security of Arms, Ammunition, and Explosives*
DA PAM 385-64, *Ammunition and Explosives Safety Standards*
FM 34-54, *Technical Intelligence,* January 1998
TM 60A 1-1-22, *EOD Procedures /General EOD Safety Procedures*

Air Force
AFI 99-114, *Foreign Materiel Program,* September 1998
AFMAN 24-204 (I)/TM 38-250/NAVSUP PUB 505/MCO P4030.19H/DLAI 4145.3, *Preparing Hazardous Materials for Military Air Shipments*

Navy
OPNAVINST 3882.2A, *Navy Foreign Materiel Program,* 23 August 1993

Other

USDOT, Transportation—Code of Federal Regulations (CFR) Title 49 Parts 100-185, *Hazardous Materials Regulations*
International Air Transport Association (IATA). See their website http://www.iata.org for additional information.
DD Form 2745, *Enemy Prisoner of War (EPW) Capture Tag*
DOD 6055.9-STD, *DOD Ammunition and Explosives Safety Standards*

This page intentionally left blank.

GLOSSARY

PART I – ABBREVIATIONS AND ACRONYMS

A

AC	Active Component
ACE	Analysis and Control Element
AFACSI	Air Force Assistant Chief of Staff for Intelligence
AFMIC	Armed Forces Medical Intelligence Center
AFOSI	Air Force Office of Special Investigations
AFSC	Air Force Specialty Code
AFTTP	Air Force tactics, techniques, and procedures
AHA	ammunition holding area
AIA	Air Intelligence Agency
AMC	Army Materiel Command
AML	Army Medical Laboratory
ATF	Bureau of Alcohol, Tobacco, Fire Arms, and Explosives
ATGM	antitank guided missile

B

BDA	battle damage assessment
BDE	brigade
BN	battalion

C

C2	command and control
C3	command, control, and communications
CAHA	Captured Ammunition Holding Area
CB	chemical-biological
CBIST	chemical and biological intelligence support team
CBRN	chemical, biological, radiological, and nuclear
CBRNE	chemical, biological, radiological, nuclear, or high-yield explosive
CC&D	camouflage, concealment, and deception
CCIR	commander's critical information requirement
C-E	communications-electronics
CEE	captured enemy equipment
CEM	captured enemy materiel
CEXC	Combined Explosive Exploitation Cell

CIA	Central Intelligence Agency
CM&D	collection management and dissemination
CM	captured materiel
CMA	Chemical Materials Agency
CMEC	Captured Materiel Exploitation Center
COMTECHREP	Complementary Technical Intelligence Report
CONUS	continental United States
COSCOM	corps support command
CSS	combat service support

D

DA	Department of the Army
DARPA	Defense Advanced Research Projects Agency
DETECHREP	detailed technical report
DH	Department of Health
DHS	Defense HUMINT Service
DIA	Defense Intelligence Agency
DNI	Director of Naval Intelligence
DOCEX	documents exploitation
DOD	Department of Defense
DOE	Department of Energy
DOS	Department of State
DTRA	Defense Threat Reduction Agency

E

EAC	echelons above corps
EOD	explosive ordnance disposal
EPW	enemy prisoner of war
EW	electronic warfare

F

FBI	Federal Bureau of Investigation
FM	field manual
FMA	foreign materiel acquisition
FME	foreign materiel exploitation
FMEP	Foreign Materiel Exploitation Program
FMP	Foreign Materiel Program
FMT	Foreign Materiel for Training
FRAGORD	fragmentary order
FSAC	Fire Support Armaments Center

H

HMTO	Hazardous Material Transportation Office
HQ DA	Headquarters, Department of the Army
HUMINT	human intelligence

I

ICE	in-country exploitation team
IED	improvised explosive device
IEW	intelligence and electronic warfare
IIR	intelligence information report
IMEP	International Materiel Evaluation Program
IMINT	imagery intelligence
INSCOM	US Army Intelligence and Security Command
IPB	intelligence preparation of the battlespace
IR	intelligence requirement

J

JCBRND	joint chemical, biological, nuclear, and radiological defense
JCMEC	joint Captured Materiel Exploitation Center
JDEC	Joint Document Exploitation Center
JFC	joint force commander
JIDC	Joint Interrogation and Debriefing Center
JTF	joint task force
JTIPG	Joint TECHINT Planning Group

M

MANPADS	man-portable air defense system
MASINT	measurement and signature intelligence
MCIA	Marine Corps Intelligence Activity
MEDEX	medical exploitation
MI	Military Intelligence
MIRC	Military Intelligence Readiness Command
MOS	Military Occupational Specialty
MSIC	Missile and Space Intelligence Center
MTTP	multi-Service tactics techniques and procedures

N

NASIC	National Air and Space Intelligence Center
NATO	North Atlantic Treaty Organization
NAVEODTECHCEN	Naval Explosive Ordnance Disposal Technical Center
NEW	net explosive weight

NGIC	National Ground Intelligence Center
NIPRNET	Non-secure Internet Protocol Router Network
NMJIC	National Military Joint Intelligence Center
NSA	National Security Agency

O

ONI	Office of Naval Intelligence
OPLAN	operations plan
OPORD	operations order

P

PCC	pre-combat check
PCI	pre-combat inspection
PIR	priority intelligence requirement
PRETECHREP	preliminary technical report

R

R&D	research and development
RC	reserve component
RDEC	research, development, and engineering center
RDECOM	Research, Development, and Engineering Command
RFF	request for forces
RSP	render safe procedures

S

S&T	scientific and technical
S&TI	scientific and technical intelligence
SALUTE	size, activity, location, unit/uniform, time, and equipment
SAM	surface-to-air missile
SASO	stability and support operations
SATCOM	satellite communication
SIGINT	signals intelligence
SIPRNET	SECRET Internet Protocol Router Network
SIR	specific information request
SME	subject matter expert
SOP	standard operating procedure
SRBM	short-range ballistic missile
SS	surface-to-surface
SSC	Soldiers System Center
SSE	sensitive site exploitation
STANAG	Standardization Agreement
STILO	Scientific and Technical Intelligence Liaison Officer

T

TACON	tactical control
TE	technical escort
TECHINT	technical intelligence
TECOM	Test and Evaluation Command
TOC	tactical operations center
TSMO	Threat Systems Management Office
TTP	tactics, techniques, and procedures

U

USARC	US Army Reserve Command
UTC	Unit Type Code
UXO	unexploded ordnance

W

WIT	weapons intelligence team

This page intentionally left blank.

INDEX

This page intentionally left blank.

FM 2-22.401
NTTP 2-01.4
AFTTP(I) 3-2.63

9 June 2006

By Order of the Secretary of the Army:

Official:

PETER J. SCHOOMAKER
General, United States Army
Chief of Staff

JOYCE E. MORROW
Administrative Assistant to the
Secretary of the Army
0618706

DISTRIBUTION:
Active Army, Army National Guard, and US Army Reserve: Distribute in accordance with the initial distribution number (IDN) 115963 requirements for FM 2-22.401.

By Order of the Secretary of the Air Force

JAMES F. JACKSON
Brigadier General, US Air Force
Commander
Headquarters Air Force Doctrine Center

Air Force Distribution: F